编委会

主　　编：王　凯

副 主 编：徐　辉　王伟英

执行副主编：史英静

编　　委：耿艳妍　李秀明　戚纤云　赵大伟
　　　　　李佳俊　丁　鑫　马　琰　张晓瑄
　　　　　张海荣　孔晓红　马诗瑶　张启璇

Editorial Board

Editor in Chief: Wang Kai

Deputy Editors in Chief: XuHui, Wang Weiying

Deputy Executive Editor: Shi Yingjing

Editorial Board Members: Geng Yanyan, Li Xiuming, Qi Xianyun, Zhao Dawei, Li Jiajun, Ding Xin, Ma Yan, Zhang Xiaoxuan, Zhang Hairong, Kong Xiaohong, Ma Shiyao, Zhang Qixuan

走近福建传统村落

中国城市规划设计研究院 ◎ 编著

北京出版集团
北京出版社

图书在版编目（CIP）数据

走近福建传统村落 / 中国城市规划设计研究院编著. — 北京 : 北京出版社，2020.10
ISBN 978-7-200-15844-1

Ⅰ. ①走… Ⅱ. ①中… Ⅲ. ①村落—介绍—福建 Ⅳ. ①K925.75

中国版本图书馆 CIP 数据核字（2020）第 165739 号

走近福建传统村落
ZOUJIN FUJIAN CHUANTONG CUNLUO

中国城市规划设计研究院　编著

*

北 京 出 版 集 团
北 京 出 版 社　出版
（北京北三环中路6号）
邮政编码：100120

网　　址：www.bph.com.cn
北 京 出 版 集 团 总 发 行
新 华 书 店 经 销
北京瑞禾彩色印刷有限公司印刷

*

880毫米×1230毫米　32开本　7.5印张　192千字
2020年10月第1版　2020年10月第1次印刷
ISBN 978-7-200-15844-1
定价：65.00元
如有印装质量问题，由本社负责调换
质量监督电话：010-58572393

序 / Foreword

2002年，时任福建省省长的习近平同志为《福州古厝》一书撰写了序，提出"福建有福州、泉州、漳州、长汀四座国家级历史文化名城，这是福建的骄傲。另外，还有许多省级的历史文化名村、名镇。"近20年来，在福建省各级各部门的持续努力工作下，全省名城、名镇、名村、传统村落、历史文化街区、历史建筑和风貌建筑等各类城乡文化遗产名录得到了进一步丰富，遗产承载的历史信息不断释放，肇始于周、跨山向海的八闽文化传统得以更好地彰显。

2012年至今，中国住房和城乡建设部界定了5批6819个中国传统村落，福建全省共有494个村落被纳入了《中国传统村落名录》，数量位列全国第六。福建还有76个中国历史文化名镇名村、125个省级历史文化名镇名村和356个省级传统村落。这些村落遗产是福建，乃至中国重要的文化遗产。它们分布在福建的山地、丘陵、河谷、平原、江畔、海边、温泉集群地、世界遗产汇聚区。无论是北方衣冠士族迁徙所孕育的宗族文化，抑或依托海洋而造就的华侨文化，都通过历史的线索和印记在传统村落中呈现。

In 2002, the then governor of Fujian Province Xi Jinping wrote a foreword for the book *Ancient Houses in Fuzhou*, in which he said "Fujian is proud of being home to four state-level historical and cultural cities–Fuzhou, Quanzhou, Zhangzhou and Changting–and villages and townships of historical and cultural significance at the provincial level." Over the past nearly 20 years, Fujian's government agencies at all levels have stayed committed to reviving the cities, townships, villages, localities, and architectures with historic significance, as well as scenic buildings. With that, more messages about historical truth have been delivered and Fujian's culture and traditions that were shaped in the Zhou Dynasty better promoted.

Since 2012, China's Ministry of Housing and Urban-Rural Development has recognized a total of 6,819 traditional Chinese villages in five batches in *Traditional Chinese Villages Catalog*. Among them, Fujian takes 494 spots, ranking sixth among Chinese provinces. In addition, the province boasts 76 townships and villages which have been recognized as state-level historical and cultural divisions, 125 provincial ones, and 356 traditional villages at the provincial level. These villages are vital cultural heritage sites for Fujian and beyond. Some are located in mountainous and hilly areas or river valleys, some overlooking a river or seas, and others on a plain or at a cluster of hot springs or World Heritage sites. The traces of the time-honored culture of all kinds, be it the clan culture bred by influential migrants from Northern China or the overseas Chinese culture developed due to the proximity to the sea, can be found in these historical communities.

历史文化遗产是不可再生、不可替代的宝贵资源，需要用心守护。与此同时，我们也深知文化遗产保护的最终目的，不仅是为人类留下珍贵的时代文明、历史记忆，还在于让公众感悟中华文化、传承中华文明、增强文化自信。那么，要让文化遗产有长久的生命力，需要让社会大众首先认识到文化遗产的价值与保护意义，从而自发地参与到文化遗产的保护活化中来。

此次，中国城市规划设计研究院联合福建省住房和城乡建设厅，组织编写了《走近福建传统村落》宣传画册，从福建全省精选了50个优秀传统村落，形成了福建多样生态环境、丰富历史文化、独特民俗信仰的典型代表群像。通过相关专家、学者的共同努力，不仅提炼出了每个传统村落的特殊文化、重要价值、传承现状，还将最有韵味的传统村落景致呈现给了大众。

此外，福建省还推出传统村落活化利用的平台——"传统村落海峡租养平台"。我们期待社会各界能参与到更多传统村落保护发展、活化利用方式的创新中来，使传统村落得以再生，历史文化得以传承，人居智慧得以光大。

Historical and cultural heritages are irreplaceable precious resources that should be well-preserved. Deep in our heart, we know that the ultimate goal of protecting cultural heritages is not just to keep alive human civilizations and memories, but to enable the general public to understand, appreciate, and carry forward the Chinese culture, and enhance their cultural confidence. To keep cultural heritages vibrant requires the public to realize what value of these heritages is and why they need to be protected and reenergized. The move is fundamental before people voluntarily offer to preserve and revive the invaluable sites.

In collaboration with the Department of Housing and Urban-Rural Development of Fujian, the China Academy of Urban Planning and Design developed the photo album *Traditional Villages in Fujian*. The photo album interprets the province's diverse ecology, rich history and vibrant culture, as well as distinct folk customs by presenting the fascinating photos of 50 historical villages. With a joint effort of experts and scholars, the unique culture, significant value, and preservation of each traditional community are identified, and more importantly, their most magnificent facets are here to stay.

In addition, Fujian launched the "Platform for the Channel Rental and Maintenance of Traditional Villages" as a way to revive these historical structures. It is our hope that all sectors of society can devote greater energy to protecting traditional villages and developing new ways to revive them. This is how historical communities can be kept alive, time-honored culture passed down, and intelligent living style carried forward.

杨保军

Yang Baojun

中国住房和城乡建设部总经济师

Chief Economist, the Ministry of Housing and Urban-Rural Development

目录
Contents

001 前言
Preface

福州
Fuzhou

002 福州·福清东山村
Dongshan Village, Fuqing, Fuzhou City

006 福州·福清文关村
Wenguan Village, Fuqing, Fuzhou City

010 福州·闽清桥东村
Qiaodong Village, Minqing County, Fuzhou City

014 福州·闽清塘下村
Tangxia Village, Minqing County, Fuzhou City

018 福州·永泰寨里村
Zhaili Village, Yongtai County, Fuzhou City

漳州
Zhangzhou

024 漳州·华安大地村
Dadi Village, Hua'an County, Zhangzhou City

030 漳州·南靖葛竹村
Gezhu Village, Nanjing County, Zhangzhou City

034 漳州·南靖河坑村
Hekeng Village, Nanjing County, Zhangzhou City

038 漳州·南靖坎下村
Kanxia Village, Nanjing County, Zhangzhou City

042 漳州·南靖塔下村
Taxia Village, Nanjing County, Zhangzhou City

046 漳州·南靖田螺坑村
Tianluokeng Village, Nanjing County, Zhangzhou City

050 漳州·云霄山后村
Shanhou Village, Yunxiao County, Zhangzhou City

052 漳州·漳浦赵家城村
Zhaojiacheng Village, Zhangpu County, Zhangzhou City

056 漳州·长泰珪后村
Guihou Village, Changtai County, Zhangzhou City

001

泉州
Quanzhou

062　泉州·安溪南岩村
　　　Nanyan Village, Anxi County, Quanzhou City

066　泉州·德化云溪村
　　　Yunxi Village, Dehua County, Quanzhou City

070　泉州·晋江塘东村
　　　Tangdong Village, Jinjiang, Quanzhou City

074　泉州·南安观山村
　　　Guanshan Village, Nan'an County, Quanzhou City

078　泉州·泉港涂坑村
　　　Tukeng Village, Quangang District, Quanzhou City

082　泉州·永春茂霞村
　　　Maoxia Village, Yongchun County, Quanzhou City

三明
Sanming

088　三明·将乐良地村
　　　Liangdi Village, Jiangle County, Sanming City

092　三明·明溪御帘村
　　　Yulian Village, Mingxi County, Sanming City

096　三明·清流赖安村
　　　Lai'an Village, Qingliu County, Sanming City

100　三明·沙县水美村
　　　Shuimei Village, Shaxian County, Sanming City

104　三明·永安沧海畲族村
　　　Canghai She Ethnic Village, Yong'an County, Sanming City

110　三明·尤溪桂峰村
　　　Guifeng Village, Youxi County, Sanming City

莆田
Putian

116　莆田·荔城后黄村
　　　Houhuang Village, Licheng District, Putian City

南平
Nanping

122　南平·建阳后畲村
　　　Houshe Village, Jianyang District, Nanping City

126　南平·邵武和平村
　　　Heping Village, Shaowu County, Nanping City

130　南平·顺昌上湖村
　　　Shanghu Village, Shunchang County, Nanping City

134　南平·武夷山兴贤村
　　　Xingxian Village, Wuyishan, Nanping City

龙岩 Longyan

140	龙岩·连城培田村 Peitian Village, Liancheng County, Longyan City
144	龙岩·永定初溪村 Chuxi Village, Yongding District, Longyan City
148	龙岩·永定高北村 Gaobei Village, Yongding District, Longyan City
152	龙岩·永定洪坑村 Hongkeng Village, Yongding District, Longyan City
156	龙岩·永定岩太村 Yantai Village, Yongding County, Longyan City
160	龙岩·长汀三洲村 Sanzhou Village, Changting County, Longyan City

宁德 Ningde

166	宁德·福安康源村 Kangyuan Village, Fu'an, Ningde City
170	宁德·福安廉村 Liancun Village, Fu'an, Ningde City
174	宁德·福安楼下村 Louxia Village, Fu'an, Ningde City
178	宁德·福安南岩村 Nanyan Village, Fu'an, Ningde City
182	宁德·福安坦洋村 Tanyang Village, Fu'an, Ningde City
186	宁德·福安秀峰村 Xiufeng Village, Fu'an, Ningde City
190	宁德·古田端上村 Duanshang Village, Gutian County, Ningde City
194	宁德·屏南北墘村 Beiqian Village, Pingnan County, Ningde City
198	宁德·屏南漈下村 Jixia Village, Pingnan County, Ningde City
202	宁德·寿宁下党村 Xiadang Village, Shouning County, Ningde City
206	宁德·霞浦半月里村 Banyueli Village, Xiapu County, Ningde City

平潭 Pingtan

212	平潭·北港村 Beigang Village, Pingtan
216	平潭·青峰村 Qingfeng Village, Pingtan
219	后记 Afterword

前言 Preface

福建，位于中国东南沿海，三面封闭重山，纵横独流之水奔腾向东入海。隋唐伊始，福建泉州便同浙江宁波、广东广州一道成为世界上最重要的港口城市。瓷器、丝绸、茶叶从泉州港起航，经过绵延千万里的"海上丝绸之路"，将古老中国的文明送达世界各地。

如今，在中国"一带一路"的倡议下，沿线国家建立了文化包容的命运共同体。福建不仅是纵贯南北的"中欧班列"通达亚欧12个国家的重要节点，也是"21世纪海上丝绸之路"的核心区。福建，再次站在了中国文化传播的起点。

福建受山水阻隔，不得不"向海而生"，包容敢闯的性格又使福建"因海而兴"。在漫长的历史画卷中，丰富的自然生态环境和多元的文化体系，共同绘就了福建最浪漫而独特的色彩。

丰富的自然地理

福建大地上，遍布着山地、丘陵，森林覆盖率居全国首位。以武夷山脉为主的闽西大山带与中部的闽中大山带纵贯东北至西南，成为支撑起福建的骨架。

泉水、瀑布自山间孕育，又一路汇聚成河寻路东去。它们编织了福建纵横的水系网络，也促使河谷、盆地和冲积平原等多元地貌的形成，其中最长、最大的河流便是从福州入海的闽江。

Fujian, a coastal province, lies on the southeastern China. It is surrounded on three sides by imposing mountain ranges and overlooks a mighty river that flows eastward to the sea. Together with Zhejiang's Ningbo and Guangdong's Guangzhou, Quanzhou, a prefecture-level city of Fujian, has already been among the most important port cities across the globe since the Sui and Tang Dynasties. Starting from the Quanzhou Port, one end of the long Maritime Silk Road, an array of products representing the ancient Chinese civilization, such as porcelain, silk, and tea, were delivered to every corner of the world.

Today, the China-proposed Belt and Road Initiative (BRI) has ensured the emergence of a community with a shared future that encourages cultural inclusion among the Belt and Road countries. As a critical hub for the China-Europe Freight Trains running north and south to reach 12 Eurasian countries, Fujian also serves as the core area of the 21st Century Maritime Silk Road, the sea route part of the BRI. Once again, the province stands as a starting point to spread Chinese culture.

Separated by mountains and waters, Fujian has to develop by exploring what the sea has to offer, and it is the open-minded, pioneering people that make the province thrive. In the long course of history, a blend of abundant natural resources and diverse culture has helped develop Fujian into a uniquely romantic place.

A Rich Natural Landscape

Home to the mountainous and hilly terrain, Fujian tops the country in terms of forest coverage. The western Fujian mountain belt that centers on the Mount Wuyi and the central Fujian mountain belt that runs from northeast to southwest form the backbone of the province's landscape.

Springs and waterfalls originate from mountains and join a mighty river surging to the east. This is how Fujian is blessed with an extensive network of waterways, coupled with river valleys, basins, and flood plains. Among all those rivers, the longest and largest is the Min River, the lower reaches of which center in Fuzhou, Fujian's capital city.

福建省传统村落分布图
The layout of traditional villages in Fujian Province

图例
Legend

- 福州 Fuzhou City
- 漳州 Zhangzhou City
- 泉州 Quanzhou City
- 三明 Sanming City
- 莆田 Putian City
- 南平 Nanping City
- 龙岩 Longyan City
- 宁德 Ningde City
- 平潭 Pingtan

独特的海洋生态

福建拥有约 3300 千米的海岸线，约等于北京到拉萨的距离。它的海域面积宽达 13.6 万平方千米，超过陆地面积 1.5 万平方千米。临海的 1400 多个大大小小的岛屿中，平潭岛和东山岛均位居中国大面积岛屿之列。

多元的文化体系

丰富的自然地理、生态环境是福建的典型特色。历代的人口迁徙则进一步造就了福建多元的文化体系。

西晋、唐宋时期，北方多次战乱促使"衣冠南渡"。中原士庶几经辗转，迁至江南地区，大量人口也随之源源不断地迁入福建，这是早期自北向南至闽的战争移民。

他们翻山越岭，跨过江河、海洋，克服了山水之难，不断适应着福建多元的自然地理环境，建立起靠山、近水、临海等多样的传统聚落群。同时，在不同民族信仰及现实环境影响下，各聚落群形成了独具特色、迥然不同的生产生活方式、建筑形态、非遗民俗和文化信仰等。

这些共同造就了福建的"福建土楼""中国丹霞""武夷山""鼓浪屿"四项世界文化、自然遗产，以及"妈祖信俗""南音""中国传统木结构建筑营造技艺（闽南传统民居营造技艺）""福建木偶戏""中国水密隔舱福船制造技艺""中国木拱桥传统营造技艺""中国剪纸"七项世界非物质文化遗产。

A Distinct Marine Ecosystem

Fujian boasts about 3,300 kilometers of coastline, equivalent to the approximate distance from Beijing to Lhasa. It administers a sea area of 136,000 square kilometers, 15,000 square kilometers more than the land area it covers. Of over 1,400 islands in Fujian, Pingtan Island and Dongshan Island rank among the large islands in China.

A Diverse Cultural System

Endowed with rich natural landscape and flourishing ecosystem, Fujian has created a diverse cultural system due to human migrations in Chinese history.

Due to wars, different waves of human migration from northern China to the south took place in the Western Jin, Tang, and Song Dynasties. After twists and turns, those Chinese, aristocratic or ordinary, from Zhongyuan, an area along the lower reaches of the Yellow River, had moved to Jiangnan, the south of the lower reaches of the Yangtze River. And Fujian witnessed a constant influx of migrants displaced by wars.

Having surmounted all difficulties along the way to Fujian and adapted themselves to its diverse natural landscape, these migrants managed to shape their communities in the mountains, by the riverside, or near the coast. And influenced by their own beliefs and the living environment, these settlers have created distinct ways of living and production, architectural styles, intangible cultural heritage, and cultural beliefs.

The achievements they together made include four world cultural and natural heritage sites, namely Fujian Tulou (a large, enclosed and fortified earthen building with thick, load-bearing and rammed-earth walls), Danxia Landform in China, the Mount Wuyi, and Kulangsu (also named Gulangyu) Island, and seven items of world intangible cultural heritage, including Mazu belief and customs, Nanyin music (a style of Chinese classical music originating in Fujian), traditional architectural craftsmanship for dwellings in south Fujian (Minnan), Fujian puppetry, watertight-bulkhead technology of Chinese junks, traditional craftsmanship for building Chinese wooden arch bridges, and Chinese paper-cut.

2012年至今，福建共有494个村落被纳入《中国传统村落名录》。这些村落形成年代较早，蕴藏着丰富的自然生态资源，保留着大量的历史文化信息，记录了福建的根基和传统。它们散布在福建省下辖的福州、漳州、泉州、三明、莆田、南平、龙岩、宁德、平潭，形成了福建丰富的传统文化遗产聚落群，是福建优秀传统文化的发源地和留存地。

平潭的青峰村，三面临海，为了生存，人们世代以海洋捕捞为业。为躲避海洋暴风雨侵袭，他们就地取材，建造起了座座石头厝。

宁德福安的廉村，穆阳溪款款流过，孕育了肥沃的土地，也造就了村落独一无二的枢纽位置。人们在这里安居乐业、读圣贤书，也在这里创造了商贸重镇的辉煌时代。

南平邵武和平村，处于闽赣关隘，商贸交易频繁。但因其地势平坦，人们不得不建造巨型城堡以避匪患，守护村落财富安全。

Since 2012, a total of 494 villages in Fujian have been included in *Traditional Chinese Villages Catalog*. Boasting a long history, abundant natural resources, and a wealth of culture, they stand to see how Fujian developed from the start and how its traditions have been preserved. As they dot the cities of Fuzhou, Zhangzhou, Quanzhou, Sanming, Putian, Nanping, Longyan, Ningde, and Pingtan, clusters of traditional cultural heritage sites were formed, representing the cradles and preserving sites of fine traditions and culture of Fujian.

Qingfeng Village is a community surrounded on three sides by water, and locals have fished for a living for generations. To guard against storms from the sea, they built stone cuos (ancient houses) by using local materials.

The Muyang Stream flows through Liancun in Ningde, making the village fertile and geographically unique. Inspired by works of ancient sages, people there lived and worked in contentment and developed the village into a strategically important commercial hub.

Situated at the link between Fujian and Jiangxi, Heping Village in Shaowu County, Nanping City, saw a booming trade. However, since it stands on a piece of flat land, dwellers had to construct a gigantic castle-style village to guard against bandits and ensure wealth and safety within.

一般来看，福建全域传统建筑分闽东民居、闽北民居、莆仙民居、客家民居、闽南民居、闽中民居、土楼、番仔洋楼和沿海石厝9大类和近30多种小类，多样建筑风格都在传统村落中得以完美呈现。

Historic buildings across the province comprise featured residential houses in the eastern, northern, southern, and central parts of Fujian, Puxian and Hakka dwellings, coupled with Tulou, western-style building, and stone cuo in coastal areas. And 30 variants and more were derived from these constructions, which collectively make traditional villages alive with diverse architectural styles.

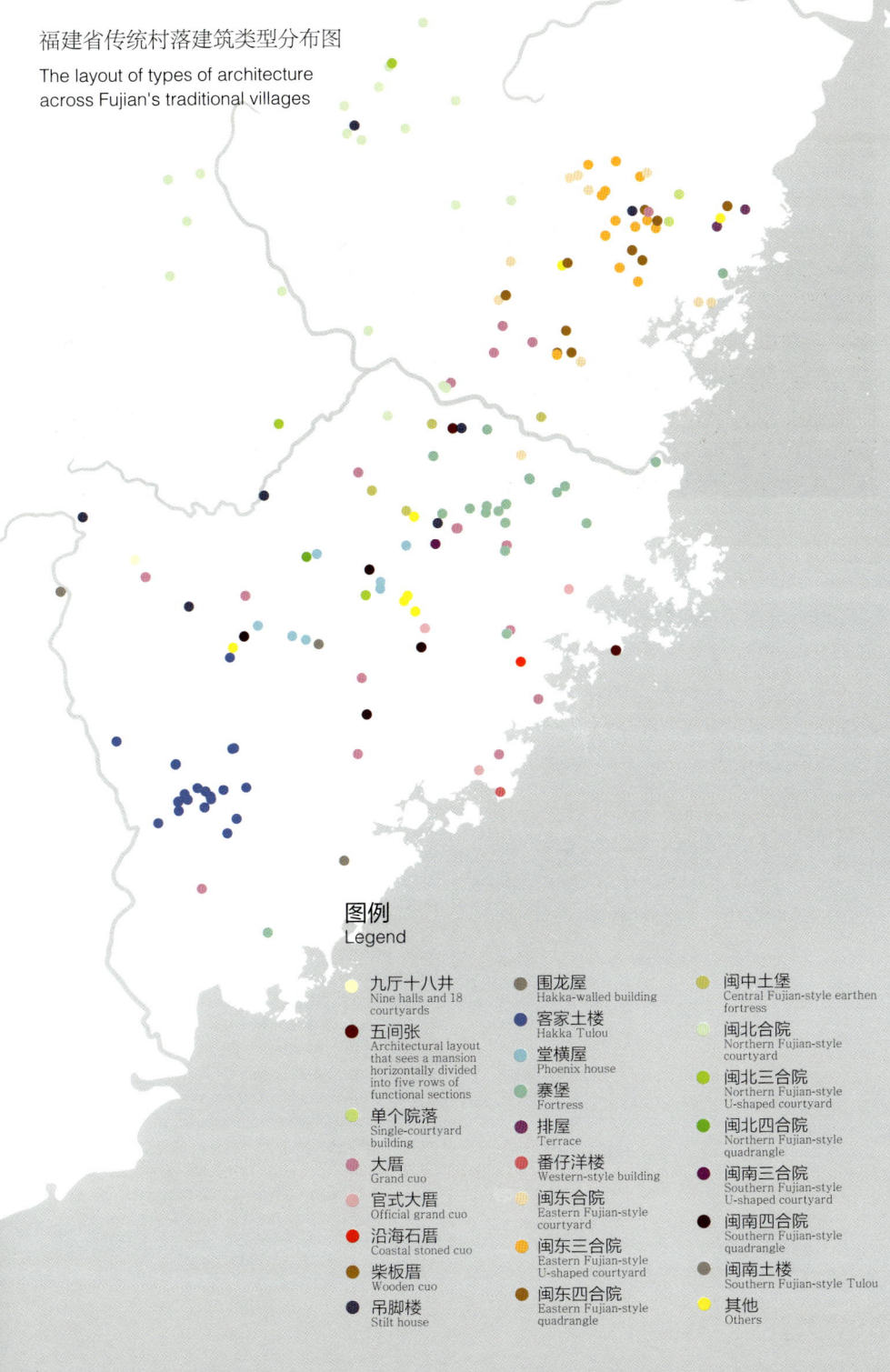

漳州南靖田螺坑村，山腰的密林间建起了五座如今的世界文化遗产——福建客家土楼。这满足了辗转入闽的客家人对家族团结、防患山匪的需求。

三明沧海畲族村，是大山深处隐秘的少数民族村寨。历史上，他们一路北上入闽，仍延续着凤凰信仰和民族融合后的生活习惯。

千百年来，中原先民与福建本土闽越人在不断融合中，创造了辉煌灿烂的多元文化。明清时期，随着闽南人"下南洋"浪潮的掀起，福建的文化则变得更为绚烂多彩。

明清时期，福建厦门、漳州、泉州的闽南人开始大规模漂洋过海，纷纷赴东南亚经商，这是后期福建自内而外的经济移民。荣归故里的闽商"叶落归根"，他们引入了先进的生产生活方式、文化理念，也带回了新的建筑风格。

Located in Nanjing County, Zhangzhou City, the mountainside village of Tianluokeng is home to five majestic Hakka Tulou, also a world cultural heritage site. For the Hakka people migrating to Fujian with twists and turns, these structures were well-positioned to unite their clansmen and fight against gangsters.

Canghai She Ethnic Village represents a mountainside community of Sanming dominated by the She people. Historically, they moved to Fujian from the further south and have stayed committed to the worship of phoenix and the ethnic assimilation practices.

For centuries, the continued interaction between the forefathers in Zhongyuan and the Minyue people, Fujian's original inhabitants, has contributed to the splendid, diverse culture of Fujian. And the culture was taken to a new level as waves of Minnan people ventured to the Southeast Asia to seek fortune in the Ming and Qing Dynasties.

At that time, a majority of the Minnan people from Xiamen, Zhangzhou, and Quanzhou crossed the ocean to engage in trade in Southeast Asia, which was the recent outflow of economic migrants of Fujian. Over years, they returned to their homeland prosperous, and with them came the advanced ways of living and production and new cultures and architectural styles.

泉州泉港涂坑村，临海而居，村民们曾大规模从事海上贸易，使这里成了海上丝绸之路的港市。座座红砖大厝，色彩亮丽，蔚为壮观，昭示了这里曾经的繁华景象。

泉州晋江塘东村，一座中西合璧的番仔楼见证了菲律宾"糖王"蔡本油的南洋故事；安溪南岩村，深山中的红砖古厝，翘尾飞檐间诉说着清代海运大茶商广博的见识；莆田荔城后黄村，60多幢具有南洋风格的华侨老宅也是几代人漂泊海外打拼而后归乡造就的建筑文化融合典范。

历经千百年，福建多元的文化以物质及非物质文化形态镌刻沉淀在了八闽大地上的传统村落中，始终为后人传承着、延续着。它们代表了多元的福建，也构成了多元的中国。

《走近福建传统村落》画册遴选了福建下辖市县最具地域文化代表性的50个传统村落，并对其进行价值提炼，引导人们由远及近，重新认识、探究体会传统村落的韵味和丰富多元的价值。画册中的村落所处的自然地理环境丰富多样，包括山居村落、临水村落、河谷村落、海岛村落、平原村落和世界遗产所在地村落。这些村落在历史文化、建筑风格、民俗非遗、民间信仰等方面各具地域特色，且在传统村落保护、发展工作中也取得了积极成果。

希望这些传统村落能让您领略福建大地的多彩，带您发现福建、认识福建、读懂中国。

As a seaside community in Quangang, a district of Quanzhou, Tukeng Village was a port along the Maritime Silk Road, with most locals engaging in maritime trade. Rows of magnificently bright red-brick ancient cuos are just a testimony to the prosperity the place once enjoyed.

In Tangdong Village of Jinjiang, a county-level city of Quanzhou, stands a featured house of Chinese and Western styles, which justifies how the villager Cai Benyou did business in the Philippines and emerged as a huge sugar supplier. And the red-brick ancient cuos decorated with featured cornices in remote mountains of Nanyan Village, Anxi County, revealed the extensive knowledge of the big tea merchants in the booming maritime trade in the Qing Dynasty. Situated in Licheng, a district of Putian, Houhuang Village is home to more than 60 historical houses of overseas Chinese, and their design has been a fine example of the architectural and cultural blend made possible by generations of overseas Chinese.

For centuries, these traditional villages have never ceased to pass down the diverse culture, tangible or intangible, that Fujian has to offer. It is they that complete a culturally diverse Fujian and a culturally diverse China.

The photo album *Traditional Villages in Fujian* selects 50 traditional villages that best represent the local culture of cities and counties in the province and identifies the value they can deliver, guiding people to re-understand and re-explore the unique charm and diverse values of traditional villages from far to near. Geographically diverse, these historical communities stand out in their own ways. Some are located in mountains and river valleys, or on sea islands and plains; some are known for their World Heritage sites; and others are featured by distinct history, culture, architectural styles, folk customs and beliefs. Different as they are, one thing they all share is the significant progress in protecting and developing what has remained.

It is our hope that these traditional villages can provide a unique perspective into a colorful Fujian and a better understanding of the province and the country.

福建省传统村落非遗、民俗分布图
The layout of traditional villages boasting intangible cultural heritages and folk customs in Fujian Province

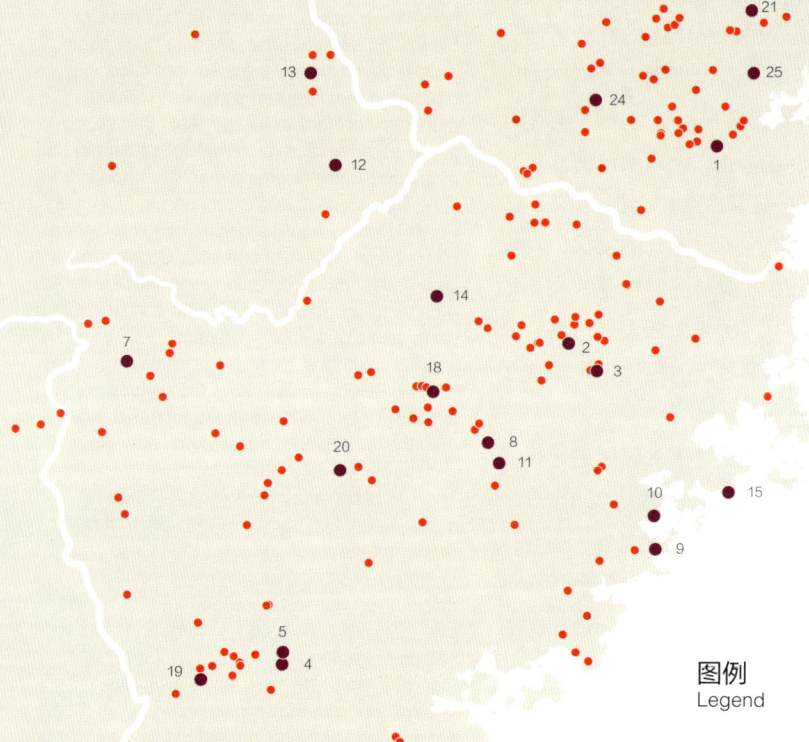

图例
Legend

● 拥有特色非遗、民俗的传统村落
Traditional villages with featured intangible cultural heritages and folk customs

● 拥有重要代表性非遗、民俗的传统村落
Traditional villages with significant and representative intangible cultural heritages and folk customs

相较全国来说，福建全域传统村落的非遗、民俗、信仰文化丰富多元且奇特。不同市县，乃至不同传统村落中的民俗、信仰迥异，各具地域特色。

Compared to the rest of China, traditional villages in Fujian feature a more diverse and distinct set of the intangible cultural heritages, folk customs and cultural beliefs. Even across the province, these folk customs and cultural beliefs are distinctive in their own ways.

1	福州罗源厚富村 闽剧	Houfu Village, Luoyuan County, Fuzhou City Min Opera (or "Hokkien Opera")
2	福州永泰月洲村 闹元宵游神、张圣君信仰、张氏祭祖	Yuezhou Village, Yongtai County, Fuzhou City Parade of the Immortals during the Lantern Festival; Zhang Shengjun Cult; Ancestor Worship of Zhang Family
3	福州永泰㟬关村 "十音""八乐"伬唱班、山歌（唱诗）、堪舆术	Tongguan Village, Yongtai County, Fuzhou City "Shiyin" & "Bayue" of Chi Narrative-singing Band; Folk Song (Slam Poem); Geomantic Omen Art
4	漳州南靖坑头村 夯土墙工艺、西天寺朝拜、四平锣鼓	Kengtou Village, Nanjing County, Zhangzhou City Rammed Earth Walls Process; Xitian Temple Pilgrimage; Siping Drums
5	漳州南靖霞涌村 保生大帝诞辰、开漳圣王、火把节	Xiayong Village, Nanjing County, Zhangzhou City God of Medicine's Birthday Celebration; Sacred King, Founder of Zhangzhou City; Torch Festival
6	漳州诏安湖内村 开漳圣侯巡安、剪瓷雕	Hunei Village, Zhao'an County, Zhangzhou City Tour of Sacred King, Founder of Zhangzhou City; Cutting Carved Porcelain
7	泉州德化双翰村 南狮表演、鼓亭公婆、木偶戏、高甲戏、南音	Shuanghan Village, Dehua County, Quanzhou City Southern Lion Dance; Drum Dance (Performed by a Couple and a Drum Worshipper); Puppet Show; Gaojia Opera (or Ko-kah Opera, a traditional folk art in southern Fujian Province); Nanyin Music
8	泉州德化高阳村 德化瓷烧制技艺、刺绣（男）、南音	Gaoyang Village, Dehua County, Quanzhou City Dehua Porcelain Firing and Manufacturing Skills; Embroidery (made by men); Nanyin Music
9	泉州惠安西头村 惠安闽南传统建筑营造技艺、襄惠公张岳的传说、惠安中派布袋戏	Xitou Village, Hui'an County, Quanzhou City Hui'an Minnan Traditional Architectural Craftsmanship; The Legend of Xianghui Duke Zhang Yue; Hui'an Nanpai Bu Dai Xi (Southern Tradition Glove Puppetry)
10	泉州泉港诚峰村 泉港区福船"水密隔舱"制造技艺、峰尾渔网具制作技艺、北管音乐	Chengfeng Village, Quangang District, Quanzhou City The Watertight-bulkhead Technology of Chinese Junks in Quangang District; Fengwei Fishing Net Craftmanship; Beiguan Music
11	泉州永春西安村 永春白鹤拳、永春纸织画、永春篾香、永春漆篮	Xi'an Village, Yongchun County, Quanzhou City Yongchun Bai He Quan; Yongchun Texture Painting; Yongchun Incense; Yongchun Lacquered Basket
12	三明沙县李窠村 沙县小吃制作工艺、肩头棚	Like Village, Shaxian County, Sanming City Shaxian Delicacies Recipes; Shoulder Show
13	三明永安龙塘村 大腔傀儡戏、打黑狮、大腔戏	Longtang Village, Yongan, Sanming City High-pitched Voice Puppetry; Nuo Dance; Drama with High-pitched Voice
14	三明尤溪京口村 茶油加工技艺、土堡制作技艺	Jingkou Village, Youxi County, Sanming City Traditional Processing of Camellia Oil Extraction; Earthen Fortress Building Techniques
15	莆田秀屿平海村 妈祖信俗文化、城隍爷信俗	Pinghai Village, Xiuyu District, Putian City Mazu Belief and Customs; City God (or Chenghuang Ye, or "Lord of the Wall and Moat") Belief and Customs
16	南平武夷山岚头村 "岚谷水豆腐"制作技艺、"岚谷熏鹅"制作技艺、竹制品编织技艺	Lantou Village, Wuyishan, Nanping City Production Techniques of "Langu Silken Tofu"; Production Techniques of "Langu Smoked Goose"; Bamboo Weaving Techniques
17	南平政和上洋村 政和白茶制作技艺、木制水碓制作技艺、陈靖姑信仰	Shangyang Village, Zhenghe County, Nanping City Production Techniques of Zhenghe White Tea; Fabrication Techniques of Wooden Millstone; Chen Jinggu Belief
18	龙岩连城四桥村 连城四堡银器制作技艺、雕版印刷工艺、锡器制作技艺、拔龙	Siqiao Village, Liancheng County, Longyan City Silverware Making Techniques of Sibao Town, Liancheng County; Engraved Block Printing Techniques; Tinware Making Techniques; Pulling the Dragon Lantern
19	龙岩永定坑头村 土楼营造技艺、客家山歌	Kengtou Village, Yongding District, Longyan City Tulou Building Techniques; Hakka Folk Songs
20	龙岩漳平东湖村 东湖米粉制作、祭拜麻阿公、游观音、穿竹马、迎仙妈	Donghu Village, Zhangping, Longyan City Production Process of Donghu Rice Noodles; Worship of Ma A'gong; Parade of Guanyin; Bamboo Horse Dancing; Welcome the Fairy Godmother
21	宁德福安桥溪村 畲族婚礼	Qiaoxi Village, Fu'an, Ningde City Wedding Ceremony of She Ethnic Group
22	宁德福安首洋村 陈靖姑信俗	Shouyang Village, Fu'an, Ningde City Chen Jinggu Belief and Customs
23	宁德福鼎翁江村 福鼎翁江柳氏月饼制作技艺、福鼎白茶制作技艺、福鼎提线木偶戏、福鼎翁江鱼灯、福鼎布袋戏	Wengjiang Village, Fuding, Ningde City Liu's Mooncake Making Techniques in Wengjiang Village, Fuding; Fuding White Tea Producing Techniques; Fuding Marionette Show; Fuding Wengjiang Fish-lantern Dance; Fuding Glove Puppetry
24	宁德古田端上村 圆瑛大师纪念日、红曲黄酒酿造技艺	Duanshang Village, Gutian County, Ningde City Master Yuanying Memorial Day; Hongqu (red starter) and Huangjiu (rice wine) Making Techniques
25	宁德蕉城水漈村 齐天大圣信仰、游神	Shuiji Village, Jiaocheng District, Ningde City Monkey King Belief; Parade of the Immortals
26	宁德寿宁亭溪村 木拱廊桥建造工艺	Tingxi Village, Shouting County, Ningde City Wooden Arch Bridge Building Techniques
27	宁德柘荣长冠村 游氏仙姑祈福、春粿粑、九天楼	Changguan Village, Zherong County, Ningde City Praying to Immortal Maiden You; Glutinous Rice Cake Pounding; Jiutian Tower
28	宁德周宁前溪村 毛竹造纸传统工艺	Qianxi Village, Zhouning County, Ningde City Traditional Handicrafts of Making Moso Bamboo-based Paper

 福州

福清东山村　Dongshan Village, Fuqing, Fuzhou City
福清文关村　Wenguan Village, Fuqing, Fuzhou City
闽清桥东村　Qiaodong Village, Minqing County, Fuzhou City
闽清塘下村　Tangxia Village, Minqing County, Fuzhou City
永泰寨里村　Zhaili Village, Yongtai County, Fuzhou City

福州 · 福清东山村
Dongshan Village, Fuqing, Fuzhou City

容纳了99间房的雄伟古寨
The Majestic Castle with 99 Rooms

历史上，东山村是永泰通往省会福州的唯一交通枢纽。这里商贸繁荣、人来人往，有驿道、驿站、商街、古厝、古寨、古碑和古桥。

交通要道的特殊位置，也让东山村匪患频发。为了防御盗匪，清代何氏家族联合筹资兴建了一座大型防御城堡——东关寨。它是目前福清市保存下来的唯一一座古堡建筑。

东关寨体量庞大，处在山腰密林深处，十分隐蔽。寨堡用黑色板瓦、鹅卵石、夯土和砖木材料混合建造，外墙坚硬万分。整座寨堡是长方形的，占地面积达4000平方米，竟拥有99间房，可以容纳近300人居住。

百年之后，东关寨依然静静地守护着东山村的人们，成了田园野趣、云雾缭绕中一抹独特的风景。东关寨之外，村落仍存有观音洋等颇具乡村之趣的自然聚落。

Historically, Dongshan Village was the only transportation hub from Yongtai to Fuzhou—the provincial capital. In the village, business is booming, and people are bustling in the streets. One can find post roads, post stations, business streets, ancient cuos, castle, monuments, and bridges there.

The unique location as the main road also presented the village with frequent dangers, such as burglaries. In order to defend against robbers, the He family of the Qing Dynasty cooperatively gathered funds to construct a large castle—Dongguan Castle, the sole remaining castle in Fuqing.

The castle, hidden on the mountainside and cloaked within a dense forest, is enormous. Constructed with black slabs, cobblestones, rammed earth, and a mix of brick and wood materials, the exterior of the building is incredibly sturdy. The castle is rectangular in shape, with a total area of 4,000 square meters, and it can hold up to 300 people in its 99 rooms.

A hundred years later, Dongguan Castle still quietly watches over the people of Dongshan Village, and the area has become a unique, bucolic landscape, shrouded in clouds of mist. In addition to the Dongguan Castle, there are many interesting, natural settlements, such as Guanyinyang.

福州·福清文关村
Wenguan Village, Fuqing, Fuzhou City

海洋孕育出的家族情结
Family Attachment Bred by the Sea

　　文关村处在福清东南沿海的半岛上，东北方向是平潭岛，西南方向为莆田的岛屿。村落三面环海，背靠山林，形成了海洋、田园、渔村、山林的空间序列，景致丰富多元。

　　村落座座石头古厝环绕分布在五连池周边。古厝或一层或两层，都是就地取材，青石、红砖、红瓦和奇特的封火山墙共同构筑起了防御海洋风暴侵蚀的传统民居。

　　凭借临海的位置优势，村落有近20%的人漂洋过海，旅居海外谋生。而大部分人则依托海洋发展了3万余亩的海水养殖业。

　　海洋给人带来一种漂泊感，这也促使村落的人们更加留恋"家族"的力量。村落的林氏家族，陆续建起了上下祖厅、东厝祖厅、绍福祖厅、新厝下祖厅、西美祖厅等众多祖厅，用以家族时常聚会联络感情，或是共商村落各项事宜。

　　此外，特色沙滩和众多无人海岛也为村落平添了一份神秘的气息。

Wenguan Village is located on a peninsula on the southeast coast of Fuqing County, with Pingtan Island to the northeast and Putian Islands to the southwest. The village is surrounded by the sea on three sides and backed by mountains and forests to the north. The sea, fields, fishing village, and mountains and forests constitute the rich and diverse landscapes in the village.

The ancient stone cuos in the village are distributed around the Wulian Pool. They are all one or two storied buildings made from local material. Blue stones, red-bricks, red tiles and extraordinary fire-sealing gable walls constitute traditional house clusters against the erosion of ocean storms.

Owing to its location near the sea, the village has seen almost 20 percent of its villagers traveling across the ocean to make a living overseas. The remaining majority in the village have cultivated nearly 2,000 hectares of land for marine aquaculture.

The ocean makes people homesick, which is the reason why villagers have a greater attachment to kinship. The Lin clan in the village has successively built Shang and Xia Ancestral Hall, Dongcuo Ancestral Hall, Shaofu Ancestral Hall, Xincuoxia Ancestral Hall and Ximei Ancestral Hall, as venues for family reunion or village meetings.

Besides, unique beaches and numerous uninhabited islets lend a touch of mystery to the village.

福州 · 闽清桥东村
Qiaodong Village, Minqing County, Fuzhou City

 错落有致的"小布达拉宫"景观
The Speckled Landscape of the "Little Potala Palace"

桥东村坐落在福州西北、闽江下游江畔，四周群山绵延，是天然的避暑胜地。

清代，在高海拔的山峦上，桥东村村民便开始了"背靠葱绿，面朝江流"的田园生活。他们建起了三座青瓦夯土古厝、一座家族祠堂。幢幢古厝连片，依靠山势，错落别致，具有层次美感，掩映在一片翠绿之中，

远看犹如西藏的"布达拉宫"。

这正是《闽清县志》里所描述的"不逊当年东山小别墅，胜占山峦之中，幽居僻壤之内，居人且耕且读"的场景。

现在，桥东村仍是避世的胜地，只保留着几条纵横小道沟通外界。每个清晨，每个午后，这里依然恬淡、清净。

Qiaodong Village is situated in the northwest of Fuzhou and the lower reaches of the Minjiang River. Surrounded by mountains, it is a natural summer resort.

In the Qing Dynasty, Qiaodong villagers embraced life at high altitudes on the mountains, surrounded by lush foliage and rivers. They built three ancient cuos with gray tiles and rammed earth, as well as one family ancestral shrine. Blocks of ancient cuos are linked together, scattered against the mountainside.

The houses, which are layered in a beautiful array, hidden amongst verdant hills, look similar to Tibet's Potala Palace from afar.

This is precisely the scene described in *Minqing Country Annals*, with people living, working, and reading in villas along the mountainside.

Currently, Qiaodong Village is still a resort, with only a few vertical and horizontal paths connecting with the outside world. Every early morning and every afternoon, the environment is peaceful and tranquil.

福州·闽清塘下村
Tangxia Village, Minqing County, Fuzhou City

 祠庙众多、信仰独特的传统村落
A Traditional Village with Many Temples and Unique Beliefs

塘下村四周被绵延的山峰环绕，潺潺溪水流淌其间，将塘下村分割成了一块块小聚落。在古杉、古松的掩映下，分散的聚落中有清代、民国建造的25座传统古厝、2座古桥和多座古庙、祖祠。

庙宇、祠堂颇多是塘下村的一大特点，有刘家垱头祖祠、叶家祖祠、林家祖祠、刘家墓洋祖祠、刘家岩角厝祖祠等。祖祠虽然简朴，但由后人传承至今，延续着一代代人的敬祖传统。

村落庙宇除了有将军庙、卢公堂，还有福建、台湾民间共同信仰的白马尊王庙。每年正月十五元宵节前后，村民便开始了热热闹闹的"游神还神"活动。

正月初六，村落的青壮年会抬着各位神像出村游乡。他们敲锣打鼓欢送神灵，场面热闹非凡。等到正月十四、十六，又由村落各神社组织"还神游村"活动，以祈求风调雨顺、五谷丰登、岁岁平安。

With rolling mountains surrounded, Tangxia Village is divided into small settlements by a stream flowing through. Behind the ancient cedar and pine trees are scattered settlements where 25 traditional ancient cuos, two ancient bridges and many ancient temples and ancestral halls built during the period of the Qing Dynasty and the Republic of China are located.

Temples and ancestral halls characterize Tangxia Village. There are Liu Clan's Qiantou Ancestral Hall, Ye Clan's Ancestral Hall, Lin Clan's Ancestral Hall, Liu Clan's Muyang Ancestral Hall, Liu Clan's Yanjiaocuo Ancestral Hall. Though simple, the ancestral halls have been carried on from generation to generation, expressing their awe for ancestors.

In addition to the General Temple and Lu Gong Temple, Baimawang Temple worshipped by both people in Fujian and Taiwan is also in the village. Every year around the Lantern Festival in the Chinese lunar calendar, villagers will organize deity statue parades out of and back to the village.

On the 6th day of the first lunar month, the young and middle-aged men of the village would carry the deity statues out of the village and take tours around the township. They would beat the gong and drums to see off the deities. It would be a lively scene. On the 14th and 16th days of the first lunar month, the shrines in the village would organize the "Deities Return to the Village" activity to pray for good weather, harvest and health.

Traditional Villages in Fujian

福州·永泰寨里村
Zhaili Village, Yongtai County, Fuzhou City

 ## 莲花庄寨里的勤俭耕读人家
The Hardworking, Thrift People of "Lotus Village"

寨里村分为上、中、下三寨。下寨形似莲花，又称"莲花庄寨"，是永泰县明清庄寨的重要代表。

莲花庄寨盘卧高山盆地间，面积达 5000 平方米。它见证了先民不畏艰险，抵御匪患的历史，也讲述了一个勤俭的家族故事。

　　建成这座大型庄寨,需要斥巨资。莲花庄寨寨门上的那副楹联"两世积俭勤,愿子子孙孙勿忘先业;一朝新甲第,庶绵绵奕奕长庇后人",就生动地描绘了寨里村黄氏家族是如何通过几代人的坚韧努力、勤奋节俭建成庄寨的。

　　如今,寨里村的先祖远去,庄寨和勤俭的传统一直延续了下来。由乡贤带头,寨里村成立了"庄寨保护与发展中心",为后代守护着这份文化遗产。

Zhaili Village is divided into upper, middle, and lower sections. The lower section resembles a lotus, so it is also known as "Lianhua Village" or "Lotus Village", which is an important representative of castles built in the Ming and Qing Dynasties in Yongtai County.

Lianhua Castle is situated in the basin surrounded by high mountains, covering an area of 5,000 square meters. It serves as a witness to people who weathered hardships and dangers, and tells the story of hardworking, diligent families.

An exorbitant sum of money was required to construct such a large castle. The couplet on the doors of Lianhua Castle "Two generations are hardworking and diligent, may the children and grandchildren remember their ancestry; a new era of successors, hailing and enduing descendants" vividly depicts how the Huang family of Zhaili Village, through generations of tenacious efforts and diligence, built the castle.

Today, the ancestors of the village are long gone, but the castle together with its traditions and values continue on. Led by the local respectable people, the village established the Village Protection and Development Center to preserve its cultural heritage for future generations.

漳州

华安大地村	Dadi Village, Hua'an County, Zhangzhou City
南靖葛竹村	Gezhu Village, Nanjing County, Zhangzhou City
南靖河坑村	Hekeng Village, Nanjing County, Zhangzhou City
南靖坎下村	Kanxia Village, Nanjing County, Zhangzhou City
南靖塔下村	Taxia Village, Nanjing County, Zhangzhou City
南靖田螺坑村	Tianluokeng Village, Nanjing County, Zhangzhou City
云霄山后村	Shanhou Village, Yunxiao County, Zhangzhou City
漳浦赵家城村	Zhaojiacheng Village, Zhangpu County, Zhangzhou City
长泰珪后村	Guihou Village, Changtai County, Zhangzhou City

ZHANGZHOU

漳州·华安大地村
Dadi Village, Hua'an County, Zhangzhou City

 ## 海峡纽带,"世遗"古村
A Village with World Cultural Heritage Linking to the Other Side across the Taiwan Straits

　　大地村拥有世界文化遗产——华安大地土楼群,这是蒋氏先民留下的珍贵遗产,更是海内外蒋氏家族后裔寻根谒祖的目的地,维系着宗族的血缘亲情。

　　居住着高山族的大地土楼群中,二宜楼、南阳楼、东阳楼尤为特别。融合中西风格的二宜楼,不仅体量庞大、设计精湛、结构优美,还蕴含着丰富的文化内涵,其中226幅壁画、288幅彩绘、349件木雕、163副楹联,还有

门楣上的西洋钟、外文标注的西洋美女画像等，十分罕见，堪称"中国南方壁画博物馆"。

土楼之外，村落有诸多庙宇。供奉玄天上帝的清代玄天阁，是村落刘氏的祖庵，祖庵部分信士后来也迁徙至台湾，每逢庙会皆会组团到这里进香祭拜。

百年以来，村落见证着海峡两岸一家亲，也延续了重要节庆里制鼠曲粿、供拜神灵的习俗。

Dadi Village is home to the Hua'an Dadi Tulou Cluster, a world cultural heritage site built by the ancestors of the Jiang clan. The community, hence, represents the destination where the offspring of the Jiang lineage at home and abroad to seek roots and pay tribute to their ancestors, in bid to forge a tight bond with their clansmen.

The Gaoshan ethnic group has dwelled in the Tulou cluster for a long time. The most prominent among the earthen buildings are Eryi Lou, Nanyang Lou, and Dongyang Lou. For instance, Eryi Lou stands as a magnificent, well-structured edifice that characterizes a blend of Chinese and Western architectural styles and cultures. It is also blessed with 226 wall paintings, 288 colored drawings, 349 wooden carvings, and 163 inscribed couplets. Those, together with other rare items, including the Western-style clock on the door lintel and portraits of Western beauties with annotation in a foreign language, are making Eryi Lou the "Wall Paintings Museum in South China."

Outside the earthen structures, the village is dotted with numerous temples. Among them, the Xuantian Pavilion of the Qing Dynasty for worshiping Xuanwu, a deity in Chinese religion, also serves as the ancestral temple of the Liu lineage in Dadi Village. Even though some of its clansmen migrated to Taiwan, they would still head to the village in groups for the temple fair.

For a century, the community has fostered ties between both sides of the Taiwan Straits and continued the time-honored custom of making the Shuqu steamed buds and worshiping ancestors in significant festivals.

漳州·南靖葛竹村
Gezhu Village, Nanjing County, Zhangzhou City

 闽南土楼里的"尊祖敬神"传统
The Minnan Tulou Carrying on the Tradition of Revering Ancestors and Deities

葛竹村是一个商与文兼具的地方。这两种气质的碰撞，让葛竹村产生了"尊祖敬神"的文化信仰。

从明代洪武年起，村落的赖氏家族就陆续建造了赖氏宗祠、太史及第、内洞宗祠、太史家庙四座宗祠。到了清代，又逐渐建起了六座家族分支宗祠，祠堂群规模之大，十分罕见。

除了供奉祖先的祠堂群，村落还建有供奉神灵的庙宇。有供奉福建本土保生大帝等诸神

031 / Traditional Villages in Fujian

的三朝宫，供奉观音、王公、孔子、真君、佛祖等神灵的贤通堂。每年农历十月到十一月，村民都会择良辰吉日敬拜答谢神明。

高山茶和枳实中药是村落的两大特色产品。如今，村落的高山茶以及枳实药材、枳实花节广为人知，吸引了大批国内外游客。

Blessed with an interplay of entrepreneurial and cultural activities, Gezhu Village fostered a culture of paying tribute to ancestors and deities.

Since the Hongwu period of the Ming Dynasty, the Lai lineage in Gezhu Village had built the Lai Clan's Ancestral Hall, Taishi (meaning "imperial official") Residence, Neidong Ancestral Hall, and Taishi Ancestral Temple. In the Qing Dynasty, another six ancestral halls were constructed, thus forming a large cluster of ancestral halls that is rarely seen.

Beyond the ancestral hall cluster, the village also has dedicated temples for worshiping deities. For instance, Sanchao Gong (literally meaning the "Palace of the Three Courts") is a temple for prominent deities, like Baosheng Dadi (a Chinese god revered most by people in Fujian); Xiantong Tang (literally meaning the "Virtue Hall") is where Confucius, princes and dukes and such gods as Guanyin, Zhenjun, and the Buddha are enshrined. Village dwellers would worship deities on an auspicious occasion between the 10th and 11th lunar months.

Gaoshan Tea, or high-mountain tea, and Zhi Shi, a traditional Chinese herb, are specialties of the village, which, coupled with Zhi Shi Flower Festival, have now become so popular that hordes of Chinese and foreign tourists can't help but hit the road to the place.

漳州·南靖河坑村
Hekeng Village, Nanjing County, Zhangzhou City

 世界文化遗产土楼聚集地
Hekeng Tulou Cluster, an Impressive World Cultural Heritage Site

　　河坑村处在龙岩永定区和漳州南靖县交界处，连接着福建两大客家土楼聚集区。

　　山谷间，14座圆形、方形土楼依次排列，形似北斗七星阵，共同组成了世界文化遗产——河坑土楼群。土楼厚厚的夯土围墙内，均建有雕刻精致的祖堂神龛，具有"外朴实内精致"的特点。

　　土楼群中有一座家族祠堂"世英堂"，它有近500年历史，兼具浓郁的客家和闽南建筑风格。这是村落独特地理位置下，客家和闽南文化相互影响的结果。

　　如今，河坑村的人们仍旧守护着座座土楼，守候着家业，也守望着这份特殊的文化遗产。

Located on the border of Yongding District, Longyan and Nanjing County, Zhangzhou, Hekeng Village connects Fujian's two major clusters of Hakka Tulou.

In the valley, 14 circular and square Tulou are arranged in the Big Dipper pattern, which collectively form the Hekeng Tulou Cluster, a World Cultural Heritage site. And behind unadorned rammed earth walls solemnly stand shrines and ancestral halls, all with exquisite engravings.

A highlight of the Tulou cluster is Shiying Tang, a nearly 500-year-old ancestral hall with a blend of Hakka and Minnan architecture. It represents a product of Hekeng's geographical location and the interplay of Hakka and Minnan cultures.

Nowadays, dwellers in Hekeng Village remain committed to keeping these earthen buildings alive for they are not only family properties, but also a distinct cultural heritage.

漳州·南靖坎下村
Kanxia Village, Nanjing County, Zhangzhou City

 ## 茶园里的双环圆土楼
The Double-ring Tulou Surrounded by the Green Tea Plantation

　　元代，坎下村先祖从龙岩永定迁徙至此。因此，村落保留至今的12座清代土楼也基本沿袭了永定客家风格。

　　"怀远楼"是土楼群中一座极具特色，且保存极好的双环圆形土楼。内外两环容纳了136间房。外环到内环通道的墙上，装饰华丽而精致，镶嵌着做工精美的绿色四方琉璃砖。琉璃砖一边有"井"字图案，一边有花形图案，寓意"锦上添花"。

　　坎下村土楼的外墙由河水中的鹅卵石和山上、地下的黏土混合夯成。在阳光照耀下，土黄色的外墙与大片绿色的茶园相映成趣，俨然一幅田园风光图。百年来，简氏族人就在这里安然度日，见证乱世，也归于平淡。

    The ancestors of today's dwellers in Kanxia Village migrated from Yongding District, Longyan City in the Yuan Dynasty. Therefore, a cluster of 12 Tulou of the Qing Dynasty in the village have basically followed the Yongding Hakka Tulou style.

    In the cluster, Huaiyuan Lou, home to 136 rooms altogether, represents a well-preserved double-ring Tulou with impressive features. Passages between both rings feature magnificently designed walls, which are made of square greenish glazed bricks with exquisite details—the Chinese character " 井 " on one end and a floral pattern on the other, suggesting good wishes.

    The exterior walls of Kanxia's Tulou are made of a mix of readily available materials—cobblestones from the river and clay in the mountains or on the ground. And while the sun shines, the earthly yellow exterior form a delightful contrast to its surrounding greenness of the tea plantation, making for an idyllic rural setting. For hundreds of years, the Jian lineage has lived a peaceful life inside the protective edifices, despite wars and conflicts outside.

漳州 · 南靖塔下村
Taxia Village, Nanjing County, Zhangzhou City

 "太极侨乡"的 78 字楹联和 23 支石旗杆
78-character Inscribed Couplet and 23 Stone Flagpoles in the Tai Chi Homeland of Overseas Chinese

　　塔下村的河流两侧，以两座圆形土楼——裕德楼和顺昌楼为中心，散布着 50 多座土楼和 30 多幢小巧别致的青砖小楼，整体形似太极图案。村落又因为历史上外出经商的侨商较多，故被称为"太极侨乡"。

　　村中张氏家族祭祀先祖的家庙"德远堂"，供奉着张氏祖先的牌位，也留存着先祖的训言。

　　德远堂前厅有两根高达 6 米的圆柱，上面镌刻了一副十分罕见的 78 字楹联。楹联用高度凝练的文字讲述了张氏家族历史上建功立业的 14 个典故，教导后人不忘初心。

除了楹联，堂前还有23支石旗杆，数量之多，难得一见。这些石旗杆是为塔下村清代以来考取功名的子孙而立，上面雕刻蟠龙，镌刻着考取功名者的辈分、等级及考取年份，以此激励后人。

The river running through the village of Taxia is flanked by more than 50 Tulou and over 30 small and exquisitely designed buildings, all of which center on two circular Tulou named Yude Lou and Shunchang Lou, respectively. Given that the layout is similar to the Tai Chi diagram and the village saw an outflow of businessmen seeking fortune overseas, the village is also known as the "Tai Chi homeland of overseas Chinese."

Deyuan Tang, an ancestral hall of the Zhang lineage in the village, has preserved not just the memorial tablets of ancestors, but also the enduring family motto.

The building's entrance hall has two six-meter-high columns inscribed with a 78-character couplet that is rarely seen. The inscription tells 14 stories concisely about how the clan rose to fame, aiming to inspire their future generations to stay true to original pursuit.

With the couplet comes a rare array of 23 stone flagpoles. They were built for those who had obtained scholarly honors and official ranks since the Qing Dynasty. Besides, they were engraved with the shape of the curled-up dragon and information about those who excelled in the imperial examination, including their status in the clan, the academic degree and the time they received it. The practice is designed to serve as an inspiration for their clansmen.

漳州·南靖田螺坑村
Tianluokeng Village, Nanjing County, Zhangzhou City

 客家土楼中的"四菜一汤"
The Hakka Tulou Cluster with a Distinct Layout

　　田螺坑村处在山腰上，依山就势分布着五座客家土楼。中间一座方形土楼，四周四座圆形、椭圆形土楼，共同构成了远近闻名的"四菜一汤"。

　　元代末年，村落黄氏先祖迁徙至此，随后在不同时代建造了这五座土楼。五座土楼——步云楼、和昌楼、振昌楼、瑞云楼和文昌楼高低错落，疏密有致，极为壮观。土楼名字和寓意自成一体，均有美好昌盛之意。步云楼，寓意"平步青云"；和昌楼，寓意"和气昌盛"；

振昌楼，寓意"奋发昌盛"；瑞云楼，取"吉祥富贵"之意；文昌楼，则象征"文运昌盛"。

"四菜一汤"中，最特别的是文昌楼。由于受地形限制，文昌楼建成了椭圆形，成了南靖县唯一一座椭圆形土楼。

历史悠久的田螺坑村也是客家民歌的传承地。一曲曲口传心授、传唱百年的客家山歌回荡在土楼间，悠长而神秘。

Tianluokeng represents a mountainside village home to a well-renowned cluster of five Hakka Tulou, with one square earthen building surrounded by four circular and oval ones, which is figuratively nicknamed "four dishes and one soup."

The ancestors of the Huang clan migrated to the village at the end of the Yuan Dynasty and started to build the cluster since then. These structures, orderly arranged yet well-spaced, just make for a magnificent view. And all their names—Buyun, Hechang, Zhenchang, Ruiyun, and Wenchang—imply happiness and prosperity. "Buyun" indicates political success and fame; "Hechang" means harmony and prosperity; "Zhenchang" suggests striving and prosperity; "Ruiyun" implies auspiciousness and fortune; Wenchang entails academic success and prosperity.

Wenchang Lou is more distinctive than the other four because it was built oval in configuration due to its geographical location. It, thus, has become the only oval Tulou in Nanjing County.

The historic village is still alive with the beauty of Hakka folk songs that have been passed down by oral impartment and sung for more than a century. The singing of these folk songs somehow lends a touch of wonderful mystery to the earthen cluster.

漳州·云霄山后村
Shanhou Village, Yunxiao County, Zhangzhou City

 临海、靠山、依江而居的村落
A Village Fronting Sea and River and with Hills at the Back

　　明代，下海捕鱼的郑氏家族为躲避台风而上岸，辗转定居在了山后村，此后便开始了临海、靠山、依江而居的生活。"山—村—田—江—海"的格局，让村落既可以迎面拥抱海洋，又能在山峦间躲避风暴的侵扰。

　　在山间峡谷里、漳江水畔、茂林掩映中，村落遗存了12座明清闽南红砖、青瓦的传统建筑，以及花岗岩石头厝、古潭、古井、古墓、古驿道、庙厝等。以花岗岩土墙围绕而成的封闭式四合院就地取材，不仅能抵抗海湾风暴，也通过"一厅一天井、四面屋顶坡向天井"的样式，达到了"四水归中""肥水不流外人田"的效果。

　　村内的两湾清潭，一个呈日形，一个呈月形，犹如日月交相辉映。如今，这个凝聚山、海、江气势于一身的小村落，也因毗邻国家级自然保护区——漳江口红树林而重新进入公众视线。

    In the Ming Dynasty, the Zheng family went out to sea and a sudden storm occurred. To escape the stormy winds, they eventually settled down in Shanhou Village, a mountainous community overlooking seas and rivers. Such a perfect geological location enables the village to make use of abundant ocean resources and rid itself of troubling storms.

    Situated in the lush valley along the Zhangjiang River, the village has preserved 12 buildings of the Ming and Qing Dynasties made of red-bricks and gray tiles, a featured architectural style in southern Fujian, coupled with ancient stone cous, ponds, wells, tombs, post roads, temples and so on. The quadrangle was enclosed by walls of granite to weather storms from the bay area, and its unique design has ensured a courtyard in a hall and sloped roofs that can channel rain to the central yard, in a way that ancient Chinese thought it could pool resources, or bring fortune.

    Beyond that, there are two ponds, clean and clear, with one resembling the sun and the other the moon, both shining brightly in the village. Today, the hilly, riverside village, small though, has again drawn people's attention thanks to its neighboring Zhangjiang Mangrove Forestry National Nature Reserve.

漳州·漳浦赵家城村
Zhaojiacheng Village, Zhangpu County, Zhangzhou City

闽南边海城堡里的"皇族"记忆
The Coastal Hokkien Castle with a Glory Past

南宋末年，为避免被元军俘虏，皇族赵氏后裔漂洋过海，来到了漳浦沿海，后定居在赵家城村。从此，这里成了南宋皇室流亡的最后栖息地。

如今的赵家城村建于明万历年间，是赵氏家族两代人耗费20多年建成的，为防边海匪患，也为纪念先祖。

村落就是一座大型城堡，其规格遵循了南宋都城的形制，有"向北望，祭先王"的寓意。堡门上，赫然镌刻的4个大字"东方钜障"，龙飞凤舞，刚强厚重，在夕阳斜照下倍显苍劲。登上厚厚的城墙，远眺城外，青山遍野，草木丛生。近看城内，清一色古砖大厝，

053 / Traditional Villages in Fujian

赵氏祠堂、家族后花园、碑林、佛庙、石塔尽显，城外城内两个世界。

内城以曾经的军事基地——完璧楼为中心。完璧楼取"完璧归赵"之意，以"璧"字缺一点隐喻没落王族饱受屈辱与复国无望的复杂情感。祠堂中，供奉着赵氏祖先牌位。古厝里，高悬宋朝历代皇帝画像，是追忆，也是祭奠。

When the Southern Song period was about to end, royal remnants of the Zhao clan crossed the ocean to the coastal area of Zhangpu in a bid to escape from the Yuan forces. Zhaojiacheng Village was where the Southern Song imperial lineage ultimately chose to settle down.

Today's Zhaojiacheng Village was built during the Wanli period of the Ming Dynasty, and it took over two decades for clansmen to complete the magnificent complex, which was designed to guard against bandits in coastal areas and pay tribute to their ancestors.

The village, a seemingly gargantuan castle-style complex, was modeled on the capital city of the Southern Song empire, in a way to worship former emperors. Its gate was solemnly engraved with Chinese characters "Dong Fang Ju Zhang"

(literally meaning the "formidable shelter blocking bandits from the East Sea"), which are lively and vigorous in terms of strokes, even slightly bold at sunset. Ascend the thick walls and you can see mountains and forests in the distance. By contrast, behind the walls lurk historical brick cuos of the same color, the Zhao Clan's Ancestral Hall, imperial back gardens, stone tablets, and Buddhist temples, as well as stone towers.

The imposing inner complex centers on Wanbi Lou (indicating the hope of restoring the Southern Song Dynasty), the once-mighty military base. The ancestral hall is where the memorial tablets for ancestors of the Zhao clan are enshrined. The clansmen hung the portraits of the Song Dynasty emperors high in the ancient cuo, as a way to honor and worship their forefathers.

漳州·长泰珪后村
Guihou Village, Changtai County, Zhangzhou City

 传承"民族精神"的传统建筑群
Traditional Buildings Standing for the National Spirit

珪后村的传统建筑群留下了不同朝代的印记，唐朝庙宇普济岩、宋代宗祠追远堂、明代抗倭遗址磐鸿楼、清代闽商的楼仔厝……每幢建筑都蕴藏着一段可歌可泣的故事，也见证了后人对民族精神的歌颂与传承。

建于唐代的普济岩内，供奉着宋代抗元英雄"三公"——文天祥、张世杰和陆秀夫。不远处的追远堂，也是为旌表曾支持"三公"抗元行动的开基祖叶棻而建造的家庙。

每年农历正月十七日，普济岩都会举行民俗活动"下水操"，至今已传承了500年。青年们光着上身，赤着脚丫，抬着神像纵身跃入普济岩庙前的水塘里，并在水中颠簸进退，演绎、再现当年陆秀夫背负皇帝赵昺投海殉国的情景。

磐鸿楼曾是明代琯后人抗击倭寇、守卫家园的阵地。这里遗存的磨坊、古井和石匾虽已古老斑驳，但那段浴血奋战的历史却让人始终铭记。

Guihou Village is blessed with a cluster of historical buildings, such as the Pujiyan Buddhist Temple of the Tang Dynasty, Zhuiyuan (meaning ancestor worshiping) Ancestral Hall of the Song Dynasty, Panhong Lou built in the Ming Dynasty to guard against Japanese pirates, the old-time Louzi Cuo for Fujian merchants in the Qing Dynasty. Behind each of them, there is a compelling story worth telling, and collectively, they stand as a testimony to later generations' commitment to the

national spirit.

Pujiyan Temple represents a place to worship anti-Yuan Dynasty heroes in the Song Dynasty, namely Wen Tianxiang, Zhang Shijie, and Lu Xiufu. Nearby is Zhuiyuan Hall, a lineage temple designated to honor Ye Fen, the forefather of the Ye clan in the village and who once supported the said heroes in fighting the Yuan forces.

On January 17th based on the Chinese lunar calendar, Pujiyan Temple would hold Xiashui Cao (Exercise in the Water), a folk custom lasting for five centuries. The young men, bare-chested and barefooted, jump into the pond in front of the temple while shouldering a god statue, and stumble in the water, reproducing the scene of Lu Xiufu jumping into the sea with Zhao Bing, the last emperor of the Southern Song Dynasty, before yielding the forces after them.

Panhong Lou was a place where Guihou villagers battled the Japanese pirates to protect their homeland in the Ming Dynasty. Although the preserved mills, wells, and inscribed stone plaques are old and mottled, the memories of those bloody fights remain alive.

泉州

安溪南岩村　Nanyan Village, Anxi County, Quanzhou City
德化云溪村　Yunxi Village, Dehua County, Quanzhou City
晋江塘东村　Tangdong Village, Jinjiang, Quanzhou City
南安观山村　Guanshan Village, Nan'an County, Quanzhou City
泉港涂坑村　Tukeng Village, Quangang District, Quanzhou
永春茂霞村　Maoxia Village, Yongchun County, Quanzhou City

泉州·安溪南岩村
Nanyan Village, Anxi County, Quanzhou City

安溪铁观音茶的发源地
Origin of Anxi Tieguanyin Tea

清光绪年间,安溪的王三言在南岩村开设梅记茶行,以制作乌龙茶闻名。从此,独具高山韵味的安溪铁观音走出深山,红遍了世界。梅记茶行的发祥地为"泰山楼",这栋已有120余年历史的老茶号,如今仍然屹立村中。

村落里散布的30余座古厝,分别对应了曾经的30余家老茶号。月寨亦是泰国"瑞珍号"茶庄老板王孝梅的发迹地。

　　峣阳古墟，依山就势，沿着当年茶叶挑夫歇脚的主街而建，是南岩村繁华时代的见证。

　　南岩村地处南岩峰群山之间，气候凉爽，早晚和雨后云雾缭绕，为高品质茶树提供了得天独厚的生长条件。这里是铁观音和本山茶的发源地，故被誉为"中国茶文化寻根第一村"。如今，全村仍有约3000亩茶园，人们传承着先祖的制茶工艺，也守候着这些茶文化遗产。

During the Guangxu period of the Qing Dynasty, Wang Sanyan of Anxi opened the Meiji Tea Shop in Nanyan Village, famous for its Oolong tea. From then on, Anxi Tieguanyin tea emerged from the deep mountains and spread across many parts of the world. Taishanlou, birthplace of the Meiji Tea Shop, is an old tea house still thriving after more than 120 years.

Scattered around the village are some 30 ancient cuos used to be the old tea shops. Yuezhai is also the place where Wang Xiaomei, owner of the Ruizhen Tea House of Thailand, started his business.

Yaoyang ancient ruins spread along a main street once thronged with tea porters at the foot of an emerald mountain. It is an eyewitness to the prosperous era of Nanyan Village.

Nanyan Village, amid the Nanyan peaks, has a cool climate and is surrounded by clouds in the morning and evening and after rain. Such an environment provides unique growing conditions for high-quality tea bushes. Here is the birthplace of Tieguanyin tea and Benshan tea, hence it is famed as "The First Village to Seek the Roots of Chinese Tea Culture." Today, there are still about 200 hectares of tea gardens in the village. Local people follow the age-old tea making craftsmanship inherited from their ancestors.

泉州·德化云溪村
Yunxi Village, Dehua County, Quanzhou City

 古道枢纽上的建筑宝库
Architectural Treasure House on Hub of the Ancient Road

历史上,云溪村是泉州德化县通往三明尤溪县的交通要塞。频繁的人员往来带来了文化的交融,也推动了建筑风格的多样性。

俗语有云:"云溪八百家,祖厝十八葩。"村内保存的"寨堡围屋"的丹山寨,古私塾"裕德堡",名扬千年的永美堂、慈济宫,千年古刹"青

云寺"，明正德年间的鱼池楼等上百座古厝依地势散落分布。从中既能看到"黑瓦粉墙长披檐，隆脊悬山木墙裙"的闽中传统建筑风格，也能窥见闽南、客家、江西的建筑元素。

此外，建筑功能亦丰富多样。明清老店铺、古桥、关隘遗址、路亭、造纸作坊及牌坊遗址历经百年仍留存。

建筑之外，云溪村的民俗活动也十分多元。千年的剪（刻）纸技艺、红酒酿造技艺、源于宋代的"迎龙灯""迎宫灯""过关煞"等活动，都是云溪人寄托美好生活愿望的隆重仪式。

走近福建传统村落

Historically, Yunxi Village was a traffic hub between Dehua County of Quanzhou City to Youxi County of Sanming City. Frequent personnel exchanges bring about cultural integration and promote the diversity of architectural styles.

As the saying goes, "There are 800 Yunxi families and 18 featured ancestral houses." Hundreds of ancient cuos in the village, such as Danshan Castle, ancient private school Yudebao, Yongmei Hall, Tzu Chi Palace, Qingyun Temple with a history of a thousand years, and Yuchi Building of the Zhengde period of the Ming Dynasty, are scattered across the terrain. From them, we can not only see the traditional architectural style of central Fujian, featuring "black tile, pink wall, long eaves, long ridge, overhanging gable roof and wooded wainscot", but also see the architectural elements of Minnan, Hakka and Jiangxi.

In addition, the architectural functions are also rich and varied. The ancient shops, bridges, passageways, road pavilions, paper mills and memorial archways of the Ming and Qing Dynasties have survived for hundreds of years.

Besides the buildings, the folk activities of Yunxi Village are also very diverse. Thousands of years of paper cutting (carving) skills, wine brewing techniques, and cultural activities from the Song Dynasty, such as "Welcoming the Dragon Lantern", "Welcoming the Palace Lantern" and "Expelling the Evil Spirits", are grand ceremonies for Yunxi people to express their wishes for a better life.

泉州·晋江塘东村
Tangdong Village, Jinjiang, Quanzhou City

 ## 海滨半岛上的白沙堤与侨乡
Baisha Dike on the Seashore Peninsula and the Hometown for Overseas Chinese

　　泉州的围头半岛，蓝天白云连接碧海白沙堤，最南端塘东村的幢幢红砖大厝，则使这幅时尚的滨海场景图更具古韵。

　　塘东村背靠群山，两面临海，隔海与金门相望。天然的白沙堤绵延近2千米，如同巨形月眉，从东南蜿蜒至西南。站在这里，你可以远眺白洋屿灯塔，也可以探到三座大礁屿，片片礁屿沉浮在海上，随潮涨潮落，蔚为壮观。

临海的区位优势让塘东村世代以海为生，发展浅海养殖的同时，也以海为媒外出讨生活。其中，最具代表性的就是近代菲律宾华侨领袖——著名的"糖王"蔡本油。他回乡后，建造了番仔楼，还兴建了公益女子学堂，让留守家中的妇女都能读懂丈夫的来信。

如今，明清红砖古厝、民国的番仔楼、近代石构民居和小洋楼，都清晰地见证了塘东村不同时代的远洋故事。现在旅居国外及中国香港、澳门及台湾的塘东村人就有近3万。

On the Weitou Peninsula of Quanzhou, the blue sky and white clouds connect with the blue sea and white sand down below. The red-brick cuos in Tangdong Village at the southernmost end give this fashionable coastal scene a more ancient look.

Tangdong Village is backed by mountains and faces the sea, with Kinmen County across the sea. The Baisha Dike stretches for nearly two km, like a giant eyebrow, winding from southeast to southwest. Standing there, one can overlook the Baiyangyu Lighthouse, and the three magnificent reef islets sinking and floating on the surging sea.

The unique location of Tangdong Village enables the villagers to make a living from sea for generations. While developing shallow sea aquaculture, they also use the sea as a channel for trade and make a living overseas. Among them, the most representative is the famous "Sugar King" Cai Benyou, leader of overseas Chinese in the Philippines in modern times. When he returned to his hometown, he built the Fanzai Building and women's school for a public welfare to teach women to read so that they could understand the letters from their husbands traveling abroad.

Today, the ancient red-brick cuos of the Ming and Qing Dynasties, Fanzai Building of the Republic of China, modern stone houses and small Western-style buildings all bear witness to the ocean stories of Tangdong Village at different times. This tradition continues, with nearly 30,000 Tangdong villagers living overseas and in Hong Kong, Macao and Taiwan of China.

Traditional Villages in Fujian

泉州·南安观山村
Guanshan Village, Nan'an County, Quanzhou City

 "下南洋"历史中的"南安第一侨乡"
Nan'an's First Hometown of Overseas Chinese Venturing to the Southeast Asia

观山村是泉州"南安第一侨乡",也是闽南红砖官式大厝的集中地。

村内依地势错落散布着30多座红砖大厝。其中,建于清光绪年间的番仔厝,从设计、施工到原材料,处处都彰显着文化融合的色彩。番仔厝由印尼商界领袖李功藏回乡建造,近代建筑大师傅维早设计,著名的印尼

荷兰裔建造师历时5年建成。建厝的原材料基本从南洋运来,运至南安仑苍珠渊港渡口,再由人工挑运到村。

除此之外,观山村的顶新厝、西金大厝、丰乾大厝等都由南洋从商的李家后嗣回乡建成。

观山村的李氏族人自明代起便融入"下南洋"的历史浪潮中,且成绩斐然。李功藏即是随父到东南亚谋生,后被推举为印尼商界领袖。当时,远航谋生为寄托生存希望,叶落归根终是人生信仰,那些中西合璧的古厝群就刻画了代代观山人"富而归乡"的故事。

Guanshan Village is the "first hometown of overseas Chinese in Nan'an" of Quanzhou, featuring a concentration of red-brick cuos in southern Fujian.

More than 30 red-brick cuos are scattered across the village according to the terrain. Among them, Fanzai Cuo, built during the reign of Emperor Guangxu in the Qing Dynasty, is full of cultural integration in design, construction and the raw materials used. Fanzai Cuo was funded by Li Gongzang, a one-time business leader of Indonesia, to honor his original hometown. It was designed by Fu Weizao and built by a Dutch Indonesian architect over a period of five years. Most of the raw materials for the construction were transported from Southeast Asia to Zhuyuan

Ferry in Luncang of Nan'an, where porters carried them to the village.

In addition, Dingxincuo, Xijindacuo and Fengqian Dacuo in Guanshan Village were all built by the descendants of Li's family who started business in Southeast Asia.

The Li clan of Guanshan Village had been involved in the historical tide of "venturing to Southeast Asia" since the Ming Dynasty with great success. Li Gongzang went to Southeast Asia to earn a living with his father, and was later elected as Indonesian business leader. They left their hometown to make a living, but yearned to return to their hometown when they were old. The ancient cuos featuring Chinese and Western architectural style reflect this belief.

泉州·泉港涂坑村
Tukeng Village, Quangang District, Quanzhou City

 "海上丝绸之路"的港市遗址
Historical Site of an Ancient Port of the Maritime Silk Road

　　涂坑村位于泉州临海的泉港区，记录着闽南人向海而生、因海而兴的故事。

　　600年前，刘氏先祖为躲避"靖难之变"，迁徙于此并开始从事海运贸易。此后，代代子嗣继承"海商"传统，至清乾隆年间，刘端弘成了彼时的泉州港首富，村落迎来了大发展，港市肇始。

　　在涂坑村，刘端弘建造了18座大厝和6间当铺。以此为基础，涂坑村逐渐形成了以刘氏宗祠为中心，南北侧依次平行排列的4座大型红砖古厝和33座普通古厝的建筑群。因海洋贸易发达，古厝群形成了"商住一体"的使用模式，涂坑港市逐渐成熟。

刘端弘还与宗亲商定"以商养文",办起了南北文武馆,重振家族文风。村落其他人也纷纷效仿,建起了众多书院、文馆和学堂。

百年后,令人震撼的稠密古厝群宣扬着豪迈的历史。"海丝港市"中的商业味道,祠堂庙宇、书院私塾中的书香气息,则依然存在,迎接新生。

    Tukeng Village is located in the sea port of Quangang District, Quanzhou City. It records the story of Minnan people who were born by the sea and prospered because of the sea.

    Some 600 years ago, the ancestors of the Liu family fled here in order to avoid the battles among members of the ruling class of the Ming Dynasty for the throne between 1399 and 1402. To make a living, they engaged in sea transportation, a business followed by succeeding generations. During the reign of Emperor Qianlong in the Qing Dynasty, Liu Duanhong of the Liu family became the richest in Quanzhou Port and the village ushered in great development and the business port began to prosper.

    During Emperor Qianlong's reign, Liu Duanhong built 18 big cuos and six pawn shops in Tukeng Village. Gradually, a distinctive architecture

cluster emerged, composed of four large red-brick cuos in parallel on both the southern and northern sides, and 33 ordinary cuos, centering on the ancestral hall of the Liu clan. Given the prosperous sea trade, these ancient cuos became flourishing commercial residences, and Tukeng port gradually matured.

Liu Duanhong also agreed with his relatives to develop education with funds from their businesses. For this purpose, he set up a literary hall and a martial arts school. Others in the village followed suit to build academies, literary centers and private schools.

Thus, a century later, there stands an impressive cluster of dense ancient cuos with an heroic history. The commercial flavor of the port, and the scholarly flavor of ancestral halls and temples and private schools still exist to welcome new lives.

泉州·永春茂霞村
Maoxia Village, Yongchun County, Quanzhou City

 荔枝树下的厝、寨与骑楼
Ancient Cuos, Fortresses, and Arcade Houses in the Shade of Litchi Trees

　　茂霞村的房前屋后，有近600株百年荔枝树，待荔枝成熟时，枝繁叶茂、红绿交织。它们是祖先建造房屋时种下的"风水树"，寓意"长寿"。荔枝树林中，田园风光里，散布着70余座百年闽南红砖古厝、民国骑楼老街、400年历史的原始古寨和石头堆砌的石城寨，呈现出了茂霞村独有的园林传统村落景致。厝、寨与骑楼，三者风格各异，留存了不同时代的闽南建筑底色，又深受西方建筑文化影响。

福茂寨被誉为"闽南聚落的堡寨"。"下灶古厝群"则汇聚了10余座明清古厝,它们有"红砖墙、白石基、小灰瓦、燕尾脊"的地域建筑风格,也有玲珑精致的砖、石、木、灰雕等内部装饰。骑楼古街曾是永春县通往外地,下南洋的必经要道。两侧有成排的民国建筑,一层的廊柱、二层的阳台栅栏,雕饰精美,样式别具一格,具有典型的中西合璧风格。

如今,骑楼老街仍保留着传统的商业作坊,走在古街,你可以感受到昔日的繁华,聆听清晨的叫卖声,坐看夕阳下惬意的人们。

At the front and back of houses in Maoxia Village grow about 600 hundred-year-old litchi trees, lush and adorned with small pink-red litchis when they are ripe. While residences were built by the community's ancestors, these trees were planted, which, in light of the Feng Shui principles (Chinese geomancy), would enable people to live longer. In idyllic surroundings filled with litchi trees lie over 70 century-old red-brick cous of Minnan style, an old-world street flanked by Chinese arcade structures built during the period of the Republic of China, an ancient fortress with a history of 400 years, and a walled stronghold of solid rock. All these make for a distinct landscape garden that the traditional Maoxia Village has to offer. The historical houses, fortresses, and arcade buildings, all featured by a unique style though, have stood for

the Minnan architecture at different times while absorbing a large amount of the Western architecture and culture.

Fumao Ancient Fortress is known as "a walled fort housing the Minnan settlers." And the Xiazao ancient cuos group consists of a dozen of historical cuos built in the Ming and Qing Dynasties, featured by such local architectural elements as red-brick walls, white-stone base, gray tiles, and cornices, and decorated by exquisitely engraved bricks, stones, timber, and limestones. The ancient street flanked by arcade houses was a sure way that connected Yongchun County to the outside world, including the Southeast Asia where people once ventured to seek fortune. On both sides stands a row of buildings completed during the period of the Republic of China, representatives of Chinese and Western styles characterized by the colonnade on the first floor and balconies on the second, with delicately unique carvings all over.

Today, the street still sees the operation of time-honored brands, and a stroll would lead you into its past glory when vendors hawking in the early morning and locals relaxing at dusk.

三明

将乐良地村	Liangdi Village, Jiangle County, Sanming City
明溪御帘村	Yulian Village, Mingxi County, Sanming City
清流赖安村	Lai'an Village, Qingliu County, Sanming City
沙县水美村	Shuimei Village, Shaxian County, Sanming City
永安沧海畲族村	Canghai She Ethnic Village, Yong an County, Sanming City
尤溪桂峰村	Guifeng Village, Youxi County, Sanming City

三明·将乐良地村
Liangdi Village, Jiangle County, Sanming City

 划分生产、生活和精神信仰区域的村落
A Village Designating Areas for Living, Production and Worship

  良地村，四面峰峦叠嶂，隐藏着上百年的庙、祠、宅、仓、桥等传统建筑。

  自梁氏家族迁徙至此，村落便严格地划分出了生活、生产，甚至是精神信仰的专属区域。纵横交错的鹅卵石小道，又将村落的谷仓区、居住区、私塾区、家庙区、廊桥区和道庵区串联起来。

  这些区域共留存了近23座明清传统建筑，完美展现了闽西北客家乡土建筑的特点。村中有供奉孔子和关羽的文武庙、梁氏宗祠、绪延厝、清代著名理学家梁奃的住所——月山公屋、由10多座粮仓组成的冠群谷仓、横跨良地溪并供奉6个神龛的水尾廊桥等。其中，冠群谷仓实为罕见，它们属于家族粮仓，或独立，或成群，仓前都垒石填土筑造平台用以晒谷，有的谷仓甚至建有院墙。

  此外，村落还是红军时期中央苏区的重要组成部分，镌刻着一段浓厚的红色记忆。

Traditional Villages in Fujian

Liangdi Village stands as a mountainous community with a cluster of over 100-year-old buildings hidden from view, including temples, ancestral halls, residences, barns and bridges.

Ever since the Liang clan settled down in the village, they created specific zones for living, production, and worship. Precisely, they had districts for barns, residences, ancient private schools, lineage temples, corridor bridges, and Taoist temples, all of which were connected through a network of alleys made of cobblestones.

These areas are home to 23 well-preserved buildings constructed in the Ming and Qing Dynasties and featured by the rural Hakka architectural style in the northwestern Fujian. Among the historical structures are Wenwu Temple, a shrine to worship Confucius and ancient Chinese military general Guan Yu, Liang Clan's Ancestral Hall, Xuyan Cuo, Yueshan Gong House—the residence of the influential Qing Dynasty Neo-Confucian Liang Wen, Guanqun Barn, which comprises a dozen of smaller granaries, and Shuiwei Corridor Bridge that crosses the Liangdi Stream and honors six shrines. A rare case is the family-owned Guanqun Barn, whose smaller granaries were independently or collectively formed, all with stone platforms for drying grains in the front and some are surrounded by walls.

Beyond that, the village also formed a critical part of the Central Revolutionary Base Area during the Chinese Civil War, engraved with a strong red memory.

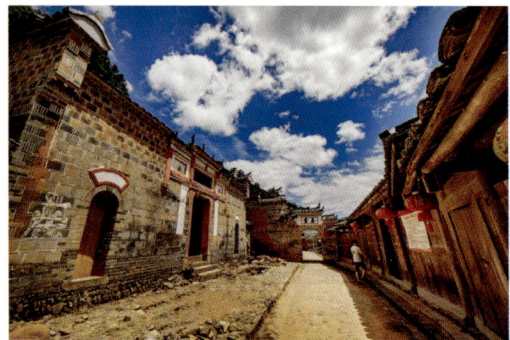

三明 · 明溪御帘村
Yulian Village, Mingxi County, Sanming City

 ## 宋代皇家赐名的村落
Village Name Given by the Royal Family in the Southern Song Dynasty

　　南宋幼帝赵昺南征途经这里，轿帘被大风吹落山野，村民捡拾归还。幼帝母亲杨淑妃为表示感谢，赐名"御帘村"。南宋文天祥遂为村落题词"山村何取御帘名，大宋南征重此行。珠箔忽因风卷去，芳名留与世恩荣。"寥寥数语，讲述的就是这个故事。

　　百年间，村落以知书达理的先祖为榜样，重视耕读传家，文风极为

兴盛，鼎盛时期全村建有 12 座书院。如今，村落仍保留着明清时期的街巷格局，传统民居、祠堂、庙宇、书院，形成了一片传统建筑群。

除了明清古韵，它还曾是中央红军驻地，留下了一段段红色佳话和诸多红色遗存。在这里，你可以追忆那段不曾经历的峥嵘岁月，看见御帘村的另一种性格。

Zhao Shi, Emperor Duanzong at the end of the Southern Song Dynasty, traveled here during an expedition to the south. Suddenly, a strong wind blew away his sedan chair curtain, and a female villager picked it up and returned it to Zhao. Yang Shufei, mother of the young emperor, thanked her and named the village "Yulian (royal curtain) Village." Wen Tianxiang of the Southern Song Dynasty wrote an inscription to mark the occasion he experienced: "Why did the mountain village take the name of Yulian? The expedition army of the Southern Song Dynasty reached here. Wind blew away the curtain of the sedan chair where the Emperor Duanzong was seated, and the village's fame is kept with the grace of the world." This is the story behind the name of the village.

Over centuries, the village encouraged residents to read books just as their ancestors did while working hard at farming. At its peak, the village had 12 academies. Today, the village still retains the pattern of streets and lanes of the Ming and Qing Dynasties. Traditional houses, ancestral halls, temples and academies form a unique architectural complex.

In modern times, the village was once a campsite for the Central Red Army, thus owning a lot of revolutionary stories and reservations. Here, visitors can recall the extraordinary years they could never experience and yet discover another part of the character of Yulian Village.

095 / Traditional Villages in Fujian

三明 · 清流赖安村
Lai'an Village, Qingliu County, Sanming City

 ## 客家多元建筑的宝库
Treasure House of Various Hakka Buildings

赖安村是典型的客家传统村落，保留了多样的明清客家传统建筑，有围屋式宅院，也有府邸式、碉楼式、棚屋式和吊脚楼式的老屋。

"彩映庚"是村内的知名建筑。它拥有典型的客家风格，由砖雕门楼、门头房、院落、上下厅合院式主座以及左侧一列横屋共同组成，样式壮阔。大门前双狮矗立，门檐高耸飞翘，檐下有极为细腻的花卉、山水、瑞兽、珍禽等砖雕，极富文人大家的气质与内涵。

村内还保留着丰富的民俗活动，有走古事、古乐坊、狮龙会、冲炮阵、赖坊武术、摆五方等，都是客家文化的缩影。

如今，赖氏子嗣延续着崇拜神灵、追思先祖的文化传统。正是这份以祖先为荣的文化自信，保护了村落的多元建筑与流传至今的民俗非遗。

走近福建传统村落

Lai'an is a typical traditional Hakka village, with various well-preserved Hakka buildings of the Ming and Qing Dynasties, including enclosed dwellings, as well as old structures in the form of mansions, watchtowers, sheds and houses on stilts.

Cai Ying Geng is a famous building of typical Hakka style in the village. It comprises tile-carved overdoor, gate house, courtyard, upper and lower hall courtyard houses and houses on the left side of the main house in magnificent style. There are tile-carved flowers, mountains, rivers, auspicious beasts and birds with rich scholastic connotations.

The villagers maintain many traditional folk activities, such as Zou Gu Shi (a local celebration in honor of Lai ancestors and Immortal Quyang), ancient music workshop, lion-dragon ceremony, running across the firecrackers, Laifang martial arts, and Bai Wu Fang (a ceremony worshiping the ancestors by placing ancestral treasures at five sites, namely east, west, south, north and the center)—all are epitomes of Hakka culture.

Nowadays, Lai's heirs continue the culture and tradition of worshiping gods and honoring the ancestors. It reflects a cultural self-confidence of being proud of the achievements of previous generations, which is helpful in protecting the diverse buildings of the village and the folk culture and the intangible cultural heritage that has been handed down through many generations.

三明·沙县水美村
Shuimei Village, Shaxian County, Sanming City

三座大型土堡
Three Big Castles

历史上，水美村不仅是沙县的重要产茶区，也是金、银、铁、铅等矿石的重要产地之一。

矿产和茶叶为百姓带来了富足的生活，但也招致匪寇垂涎。为此，人们建造了牢固的防御性建筑——土堡。土堡以防御为主，居住为辅，分布在群山密林间，隐蔽性极强。

水美村有双吉、双兴、双元三个土堡，呈"品"字形排列，分别建于清道光、咸丰和同治年间。其中，双吉堡地势最高，可以纵览全境；双兴堡更具生活气息；双元堡的规模最为宏大。

古堡依托自然地势，高低错落。内外设有炮楼、枪眼、瞭望窗、护厝、跑马廊、碉式角楼等，共同构成了一个完备的军事防御系统，便于观察、攻打堡外匪徒。古堡外围还有层层梯田，供古堡内人们的生活之需。

如今，没有土匪侵扰，古堡的防御功能不再必要，但村落的峥嵘岁月依然珍存于堡内，直至今日。

Historically, Shuimei Village was not only an important tea production area in Shaxian County, but also one of the important production areas of gold, silver, iron, lead and other ores.

These all brought the people an affluent life, but also attracted the attention of bandits. For self-protection, the local people built strong defensive buildings known as "earthen castles", which were also used as residences. They are distributed among the mountains and dense forests with strong concealment.

Shuimei Village has three earthen castles—Shuangji, Shuangxing and Shuangyuan, arranged in the structure of three squares laid out in the shape of "品" in Chinese. They were built in the Qing Dynasty during the reigns of the Emperors Daoguang, Xianfeng and Tongzhi respectively. Among them, Shuangji has the highest location, providing a bird's eye view of the whole area; Shuangxing is permeated with a strong breath of life; and Shuangyuan is the largest.

The ancient earthen castles are scattered layer by layer, adapted to the natural terrain. There are many turrets, gun holes, lookout windows, guard houses, horse training galleries

and blockhouses, etc. which together constitute a complete military defense system against the bandit menace. There are many terraces around the castle catering for people's daily life activities.

Today, there is no bandits to threaten, and the defense function of these buildings is no longer necessary. However, the extraordinary years of the village are still treasured in the castles.

三明 · 永安沧海畲族村
Canghai She Ethnic Village, Yong'an County, Sanming City

闽中百年畲族村寨
A Century-old She Ethnic Village in Central Fujian

沧海畲族村是永安青水畲族乡9个保存完好的畲族民族村之一，畲族人口占95%以上，民族风情极其浓厚。

嘹亮的畲族山歌、诱人的特色美食、独具风格的传统建筑和丰富多彩的民俗活动，共同构成了一个鲜活的"生态博物馆"。

村落的代表性建筑龙长坊，又名"州司马第"，意为"司马官的府邸"，由清代嘉庆皇帝赐名，距今已有200多年历史。建于乾隆元年的化龙桥，集桥、庙宇、戏台为一体，由整木建造而成，结构特色

鲜明。

　　每年农历三月初七，村民都会穿着传统的畲族服装，在化龙桥举办隆重的民俗庙会活动。家家户户端来自制的"创意美食""摆盘"，作为供品祭祀。桥上人头攒动，热闹非凡。

Canghai She Ethnic Village is one of the nine well-preserved ethnic community in Qingshui She Ethnic Township of Yong'an County. More than 95% of the villagers claim She origins, and the ethnic customs here are extremely strong.

Loud and clear She folk songs, attractive characteristic food, unique traditional architecture and various folk activities constitute a living "Ecological Museum."

The representative building, Longchangfang, also known as "Zhousima's (meaning "Marshal") Mansion", was named by Emperor Jiaqing of the Qing Dynasty. It has a history of more than 200 years. The Hualong Bridge, built in the first year of Qianlong's rein, integrates the functions of bridge, temple and theater. It is made of wood, with distinctive structural features.

On the seventh day of the third lunar month every year, villagers will wear traditional She costumes and hold a grand folk temple fair on Hualong Bridge. Home-made food and dishes are placed and offered as offerings. The bridge is bustling with people then.

Traditional Villages in Fujian

三明 · 尤溪桂峰村
Guifeng Village, Youxi County, Sanming City

 弥漫着桂花香的商贸重镇
Business Center Scented with Sweet Osmanthus

桂峰村从北宋蔡氏迁徙至此，便开始广种桂花树，遂名"桂峰"。每到秋天，桂花飘香，大山间、溪流畔，家家户户都浸润在一片馨香之中。

桂峰村位于三明至福州的官道沿线，历史上往来官吏、商人和艄公颇多，村落亦不乏借此经商发财者。明末清初，村落步入商贸发展的黄金期。自此，以一条商业街为轴线，村落逐渐建起了蔡氏宗祠、蔡氏祖庙、步云楼、武举厝、玉泉书斋、清代茶楼、石狮厝、楼坪厅大厝等精美的传统建筑。其间装饰、雕刻精湛，壁画、彩绘栩栩如生。

如今，桂峰村昔日的繁华虽远

去，但村落仍延续着传统的春、秋、冬三季祠堂祭祖惯例。行祭当天，村落蔡氏宗亲会聚集在祠堂里，盛装、祭品、祭词、鸣鼓、跪拜，每一个细节都显得格外隆重。

In the Northern Song Dynasty, the Cai family moved to what is Guifeng Village today. They began to plant osmanthus trees on the mountain slopes, by the stream and in other open areas. Every autumn, the sweet smell of osmanthus fills the air.

Guifeng Village is located on the official road from Sanming to Fuzhou. In history, many officials, businessmen and boatmen traveled along the route and many villagers took the chance to develop business. At the turn of the Ming Dynasty and the Qing Dynasty, the village entered its golden period of commercial development. With money pouring in, a commercial street was built flanked by exquisite traditional buildings such as the ancestral hall and the ancestral temple of the Cai family, Buyun Building, Wuju Cuo, Yuquan Academy, tea house of the Qing Dynasty, Shishicuo, and Loupingtingcuo. The decoration and sculpture of these buildings are fine, and the murals and paintings are lifelike.

Today, the former prosperity of the village has gone, but the traditional ancestral worship practices in spring, autumn and winter have been passed down. On the day of the sacrificial ceremony, the Cai clan will gather in the ancestral hall, where they will don traditional dress, offer sacrifices, deliver sacrificial words, beat drums and kneel down to worship the deities and ancestors, with every detail being particularly solemn.

Traditional Villages in Fujian

莆田

荔城后黄村　Houhuang Village, Licheng District, Putian City

莆田 · 荔城后黄村
Houhuang Village, Licheng District, Putian City

著名的"荔城区华侨第一村"
The Most Famous Village of Overseas Chinese in Licheng District

  后黄村位于莆田东部沿海,毗邻绵长的海岸线。

  临海的区位滋生了远航的梦想,村落逐渐形成了去海外谋生的传统。因此,海外建筑风格也影响了村落风貌。

  后黄村有60多幢百年华侨老宅,都是由当时归国华侨所建。它们中西合璧,彰显了南洋风韵,也烙上了莆仙性格。

  一处古宅门前的楹联十分抢眼,"漂洋过海求生计,含辛茹苦建家园"。寥寥数语道出了历代后黄村人远赴南洋的创业故事。

如今，后黄村仍有近千人漂洋过海，到东南亚的印度尼西亚、新加坡等地工作，延续着先祖面朝大海、胸怀广阔天地的拼搏精神。村落还通过修缮、改造特色华侨民居，吸引了更多人的关注，让那些在异国他乡拼搏的华侨们的故事广为人知。

  Houhuang Village is located on the east coast of Putian, adjacent to the long coastline.

  The coastal location breeds the voyage dream of the villagers, cultivating a tradition among them of making living overseas over time. In return, the influence of the overseas architectural style on the village's landscape can be seen here and there.

  There are over 60 buildings with centuries of history in the village, which were all built then by overseas Chinese who returned to their homeland. They are the perfect integration of the Chinese and the Western cultural elements and manifest the charm of Southeast Asia and the personality of Putian.

A couplet on the door of an ancient residence is very eye-catching—it reads "Going across the sea for making a living and gritting teeth for building a home." With only a few words, it tells the venture stories of the previous generations of the villagers who have traveled a long way to Southeast Asia.

Today, nearly a thousand Houhuang people still travel across the ocean to work in Southeast Asia countries like Indonesia and Singapore, continuing their ancestors' open and broad mind and the determined spirits. The village has also attracted more attention after repairing and renovating overseas Chinese's dwellings with distinct features, making their stories widely known.

南平

建阳后畲村　Houshe Village, Jianyang District, Nanping City
邵武和平村　Heping Village, Shaowu County, Nanping City
顺昌上湖村　Shanghu Village, Shunchang County, Nanping City
武夷山兴贤村　Xingxian Village, Wuyishan, Nanping City

南平 · 建阳后畲村
Houshe Village, Jianyang District, Nanping City

 ## 武夷岩茶古道上的莲花圣地
A Lotus-filled Attraction on the Ancient Route of Wuyi Rock Tea

后畲村不仅是福建武夷岩茶古道上的重要枢纽，更是北宋理学家周敦颐笔下《爱莲说》的故地。

后畲村是中国传统理学文化的重要传承地。村落的"周"姓，为周敦颐后裔。周氏家族迁徙于此，便开始广种莲花。直到今天，我们仍能在村中看到大片的莲花。它们在晨光的照耀下，颇有"出淤泥而不染，濯清涟而不妖"的清爽美感。

以"莲"为榜样,清代,村落考取功名者达数百人,得到了"功名村"的美誉。同时,村里遗存的座座明清传统建筑也诉说着莲花的美德与品质。其中,最重要的就是雕有"理学渊源"的古祠牌坊和古祠遗址上重建的"爱莲堂"。古祠牌坊庄严古朴,细节处石雕精致万分、栩栩如生。石牌坊百年矗立,教导后人传承千年"爱莲"遗风。

如今,周氏族人仍不忘莲花精神,筹资重建了"爱莲堂",建造了周敦颐纪念馆,并定期举办纪念活动。

123 / Traditional Villages in Fujian

As a vital hub on the ancient route of Wuyi rock tea in Fujian Province, Houshe Village is the very site depicted in the poetic essay *Ode to the Lotus Flower* by Zhou Dunyi, a Chinese philosopher and pioneering Neo-Confucian thinker during the Northern Song Dynasty.

Houshe Village has been an important place to revive Neo-Confucian culture as the Zhou clan in the village is the philosopher's offspring. They have started growing the lotus ever since their settlement in Houshe Village. And thanks to their effort, the village is still alive with a greenish sheet of the lotus, and on a sunny morning, people would probably find the appealing lotus "unstained despite rising from the ooze, and modest though baptized by ripples", just as the ancestor did.

Inspired by the lotus spirit, hundreds of villagers obtained either a scholarly honor or an official rank in the Qing Dynasty, making Houshe a renowned village of scholars and officials. Beyond that, the ancient buildings dating back to the Ming and Qing Dynasties are the epitome of how the lotus survives and thrives. Among them, the ancient memorial archway engraved with

Chinese characters "Li Xue Yuan Yuan" (meaning the cradle of Neo-Confucianism) and Ailian Hall built on the site of a historic ancestral hall carry most significance. Alive with delicate engravings, the time-honored, imposing memorial archway stands tall as a reminder of promoting the lotus spirit for generations to come.

Today, to renew the lotus spirit, members of the Zhou clan have rebuilt Ailian Hall, and established a museum in memory of Zhou Dunyi where regular commemorative activities are held.

南平·邵武和平村
Heping Village, Shaowu County, Nanping City

 明代城堡里的"福建第一街"
Fujian's Most Renowned Street in the Castle Built in the Ming Dynasty

和平村坐落于出省关隘愁思岭，是福建通往江西的咽喉要道。明清时期，这里就是重要的商贸和文化交流节点，也是兵家必争之地。

贸易繁荣，经济发达，促使这里匪患频发。和平村地势平坦，易攻难守，于是，民间自发集资建造了城堡以抵御匪患。城堡有4个主城门，连接城门的城墙用河里的鹅卵石砌筑，固若金汤。自此，城外匪患常在，城内却繁华依旧。

因为城堡的守护，这里遗存了近300幢明清传统建筑，有聚奎塔、谯楼、大夫第、书院、衙门、祠堂、义仓等，

类型多样，融合了闽北建筑风格和徽派建筑元素，留下了文化交融的痕迹。其中，有12座建筑已被认定为"全国重点文物保护单位"。城堡内，贯穿南北的青石板古街及两侧鳞次栉比的商铺、纵横交错的石巷子，仍保留了当年"福建第一街"的风韵。

经济繁荣带来文化繁盛，南宋理学大师朱熹、北宋哲学家杨时都曾在这里讲学，留下了诸多经典故事。

Located at the ridge of Chousiling, Heping Village serves as a critical passage leading to the neighboring province of Jiangxi. Since the Ming and Qing Dynasties, the village has been not only a hub for commercial and cultural exchanges, but also a stronghold of military importance.

The village was plagued by bandits due to the economic and trade boom. And since it stands on a piece of flat land, easy to attack yet hard to defend, locals voluntarily financed to construct a castle-style building to guard against those gangsters. The castle has four main gates, with their formidable walls made of cobblestones. Since then, the prosperity inside the castle has remained despite recurrent chaos associated with bandits outside.

Because of the formidable castle, nearly 300 buildings dating back to the Ming and Qing Dynasties have been well-preserved. Here, a blend of culture and architecture of northern Fujian and Anhui's Huizhou can be found in various buildings, such as Jukui Tower, watchtower, Dafudi mansion, ancient academy, yamen (the administrative office or residence of a local bureaucrat or mandarin in imperial China), ancestral hall, and charity granary. Among them, 12 have been designated as national key cultural relics protection units. Inside the castle is an

ancient limestone street linking south to north, flanked by rows of stores and networks of stone-paved alleys. All this made the street the envy of Fujian.

The economic boom fostered cultural prosperity. Zhu Xi, the most influential Chinese philosopher in Neo-Confucianism in the Southern Song Dynasty, and Yang Shi, a philosopher in the Northern Song Dynasty, once imparted words of wisdom in the village, leaving many classic stories.

南平 · 顺昌上湖村
Shanghu Village, Shunchang County, Nanping City

"齐天大圣"文化信仰的发祥地
The Cradle of the Monkey King Culture

  上湖村处于国家级风景名胜区宝山内。宝山地势险峻、气候温润，山峦雾海涵养了百年红豆杉、千年银杏树和万亩毛竹林。

  茂林之中有猴群，高山之上有古刹。猴群连同元代的宝山寺，以及其附属遗迹——南天门和双圣庙，让"神猴文化"成了宝山的重要标签。掩映于葱郁山间的上湖村也因此被视为"齐天大圣"文化信仰的发祥地。

  上湖村至今保留了较为完整的明清传统建筑群和古井、古廊桥等。

  每年农历七月十七，这里都会举行十分隆重的"齐天大圣圣诞庆典"，吸引着来自东南亚各地的虔诚信徒。

Shanghu Village is situated in the Baoshan National Scenic Area, a steep, mountainous area, which is home to the century-old taxus chinensis, the millennium-old ginkgo, and a vast moso bamboo forest due to its humid and foggy weather.

Among the thriving forest dwell hordes of monkeys, and at the mountain peak stands the ancient Baoshan Temple, constructed in the Yuan Dynasty. The temple and its relics—the Southern Gate of Heaven and the Twin Sages Temple, along with these monkeys are critical assets to promote the culture of the deity. Situated in this verdant area, Shanghu Village is thus viewed as the cradle of the Monkey King culture.

Even now, the complexes, wells, and corridor bridges that were built in the Ming and Qing Dynasties remain well-preserved in the village.

Every year, many Southeast Asian believers would join the villagers to celebrate the birth of the Monkey King on July 17th based on the Chinese lunar calendar.

南平 · 武夷山兴贤村
Xingxian Village, Wuyishan, Nanping City

 ## 武夷山文化遗产中的"理学之邦"
Neo-Confucianism in Wuyishan Cultural Heritage

兴贤村是南平五夫镇"邹鲁渊源""理学之邦"的代表,更是武夷山世界文化和自然遗产的重要组成部分。

1700多年间,兴贤村成就了北宋词人柳永、"湖湘学派"创始人胡安国,南宋抗金名将刘韐、刘子羽,理学大师朱熹等无数文人墨客、理学宗师,造就了"理学之邦"的美誉。兴贤村古街上的朱子社仓、五贤井、节孝坊等众多历史文化遗迹,无不向人们昭示着这里浓厚的理学文化底蕴。

村中最为著名的建筑有兴贤书院和刘氏家祠。兴贤书院,意为"兴贤育秀、继往开来",由南宋胡宪、朱熹两代理学大师先后建造,并在此讲学传道。忠义世家

刘氏家族，亦启朱熹之道学，家祠门楼砖雕艺术精湛，祠门上方更嵌刻有御赐的"宋儒"二字，彰显了刘家在宋代的文学地位。

　　智慧累积影响了兴贤村的后人，人们以传承的"龙鱼戏"，去告慰、回馈先祖，也为祈求国泰民安。

Xingxian Village is the representative of the Zhou Dynasty and Shang Dynasty culture in Wufu Town, Nanping City. It is also the representative of Neo-Confucianism. It is an important part of Wuyishan's world cultural and natural heritage.

For over 1,700 years, Xingxian Village has nurtured many people noted in Chinese history, including Liu Yong, a poet of the Northern Song Dynasty; Hu Anguo, the Confucian scholar who founded the Huxiang School; Generals Liu Ge and Liu Ziyu, famous for their resistance against the Jin invaders during the Southern Song Dynasty; Zhu Xi, the master of Neo-Confucianism; and the village earned the reputation of "Home of Neo-Confucianism." Many historical and cultural sites flanking the ancient street of Xingxian Village tell the rich cultural foundation of Neo-Confucianism that emerged and prospered here, including Zhuzi Charitable Granary, Wuxian Well and the Arch of Chastity and Filial Piety.

The most famous buildings in the village are Xingxian Academy and Liu Clan's Ancestral Hall. Xingxian Academy aimed to "cultivate talents, carry forward the past and open up the future." It was built by Hu Xian and Zhu Xi of the Southern Song Dynasty who both preached here. The loyal Liu family also inspired Zhu Xi's Neo-Confucianism. The brick carving art of the ancestral hall is exquisite. The word "Song Confucianism" is engraved on the top of the ancestral hall gate, which shows the literary status of the Liu family in the Song Dynasty.

These ancient talents have exerted great influence on the descendants of Xingxian Village. People of later generation inherited the wisdom of their ancestors, creating a scene of "Dragon Fish Play" in return to comfort and memorize the ancestors and pray for peace of the country and the people.

137 / Traditional Villages in Fujian

龙岩

连城培田村	Peitian Village, Liancheng County, Longyan City
永定初溪村	Chuxi Village, Yongding District, Longyan City
永定高北村	Gaobei Village, Yongding District, Longyan City
永定洪坑村	Hongkeng Village, Yongding District, Longyan City
永定岩太村	Yantai Village, Yongding County, Longyan City
长汀三洲村	Sanzhou Village, Changting County, Longyan City

龙岩·连城培田村
Peitian Village, Liancheng County, Longyan City

 福建客家庄园的典范
A Typical Hakka Manor in Fujian

　　培田村是一个拥有 800 多年历史的传统村落,也是中国客家庄园的典范。

　　村落千米古街两侧的街巷里,遗存了大量明清建筑。区别于客家土楼,这里依山分布着 30 余幢"九厅十八井"风格的传统建筑,高堂华屋、商旅驿站、21 座宗祠、6 个书院、5 个庵庙和 2 座圣赐跨街牌坊共同勾勒出一幅明清重镇图。

　　双灼堂堪称培田村传统建筑的代表。厅堂的屏风、窗扇、梁头、雀替等构件雕刻精细,图案惟妙惟肖。尤其是堂前 8 块精美的窗扇,每扇浮雕一个字,连起来即为"礼、义、廉、耻、孝、悌、忠、信",引导后人以德治村,以德持家。

　　容膝居是培田村最小巧玲珑的传统建筑,典自汉代韩婴《韩诗外传》:"今如结驷列骑,所安不过

容膝"。它规模虽小，却是培田村"崇文重教"的体现。这里曾是清代村落的女子学堂，也是革命年代的女干部培训班所在地。

如今，在古老的村落里，人们传承着游公太、春耕节等特色民俗活动，也依托自身的文化资源禀赋，推动着村落保护与旅游发展。

Boasting a history of over 800 years, Peitian Village is an epitome of Chinese Hakka manors.

A one-thousand-meter-long ancient street is flanked by alleys, which lead to numerous buildings built in the Ming and Qing Dynasties. Unlike Hakka Tulou, the village is home to more than 30 traditional mansions in the style of "nine halls and 18 wells" along the mountains. magnificent manors, post stations, 21 ancestral halls, six ancient academies, five Buddhist temples, and two memorial archways presented by emperors together constitute a strategically critical community in the Ming and Qing Dynasties.

Shuangzhuo Tang, an old-time hall, stands out among the historical buildings in the village. The screens, sashes, beam heads, and sparrow braces decorating the hall remain alive with the beauty of their exquisite engravings and lifelike patterns. In front of the hall are eight superb sashes inscribed with Chinese characters: Li (etiquette), Yi (righteousness), Lian (integrity), Chi (disgrace), Xiao (filial piety), Ti (respect for the elderly), Zhong (loyalty), and Xin (commitment), in order to encourage future generations to govern the village and their household by the rule of virtue.

Inspired by the verse "the small place can allow us to sit only, though we have a large display of troops" from *Han Shi Wai Zhuan* (Illustrations of the Didactic Application of the Classic of Songs) by Han Ying, a Confucian scholar in the Han Dynasty, Rongxi House (a small place to live in), the tiniest historical building in the village, earned its name. As a symbol of how locals value culture and education, it once was a place where female dwellers received education in the Qing Dynasty and women cadres were trained during the revolutionary times.

Today, the ancient village still plays host to such featured folk customs as Tour of Gong Tai (the king of Fujian), and the Spring Farming Festival. And blessed with quality cultural resources, the community has devoted greater energy to village protection and tourism development.

龙岩·永定初溪村
Chuxi Village, Yongding District, Longyan City

 梯田尽头的田园人家
A Village Situated at the End of the Terrace Fields

初溪村处处透露着一种田园牧歌式的野趣和情调。

村落周围高山逶迤起伏，山上苍松茂林，绿树成荫，增添了浓重的自然色彩。沿着山脉，200亩成片的层层梯田舒展开来。它们由高到低错落有致，像是从高山上流下来的琴弦，在四季变换着彩色的乐谱。

梯田尽头就是初溪村，它由一座座圆形、方形土楼组成。土楼沿溪水两畔依次排开，以梯田为背景，又掩映在葱郁的山林间，共同构成了一幅恬静的田园山居图。

如今，每到金秋时节，梯田就会变成灿灿的金黄色。人们上山耕田、下山生活，犹如画中的人，过得悠然自得。

    Chuxi Village reveals an idyllic wildness and sentiment here and there.

    Surrounded by rugged mountains with thick pines and shady trees, the village is completely immersed in the nature. Along the mountains, about 13 hectares of terraced fields stretch out. They are scattered from high to low, like strings flowing down from high mountains, changing the colorful music in the four seasons.

    Chuxi Village, situated at the end of the terrace fields, consists of a cluster of round and square Tulou. These Tulou sites line up along the bank of the stream, with the terrace fields as the background and hidden in the lush mountains and forests, which together constitute a picture of peaceful rural mountain dwelling.

    Nowadays, the terrace fields will turn into golden yellow in every autumn. People go up to the mountains to plow the fields and live down the mountains, just like the people in the pictures, living an easy and peaceful life.

龙岩 · 永定高北村
Gaobei Village, Yongding District, Longyan City

客家土楼"圆楼之王"的故乡
Home to "King of Round Tulou"

　　高北村是一个客家村落。客家人讲究家族团结。为了共同抵御匪徒，他们建起了集防御和居住于一体的客家土楼。

　　高北村由46座集中连片的圆形、方形客家土楼组成。这些土楼是联合国教科文组织认定的世界文化遗产。

　　土楼群中有一座"圆楼之王"——承启楼，高四层，由内外四座同心环形建筑组成，共402间房屋，规模十分宏大。为了建造这座土楼，从明代开始，花了三代人整整81年的时间。

　　承启楼一直都是村落的地标性建筑。每到元宵节，舞龙灯民俗都会在这里登场。长长的龙灯舞动着身躯，在黑夜中闪烁着光芒，穿梭在硕大的土楼圆圈里。

Gaobei is a Hakka village. The Hakka people values family unity. In order to fend off gangsters together, they built Hakka Tulou, a combination of defense and residence.

Gaobei Village consists of 46 contiguous round and square Hakka Tulou, which are inscribed by UNESCO as world cultural heritage.

Among them, Chengqi Tulou is regarded as the "King of Round Tulou." The four-story building is composed of four concentric circular buildings, and is made up of more than 400 rooms on a grand scale. It took three generations 81 years to build, beginning in the Ming Dynasty.

Chengqi Tulou has always been a landmark in the village. Every Lantern Festival, there will be a folk show of dragon dance. The dance team mimics the supposed movements of the long flexible figure of a shining dragon along the great circle of the Tulou.

龙岩·永定洪坑村
Hongkeng Village, Yongding District, Longyan City

中西合璧的客家土楼——振成楼
Zhencheng Tulou—a Combination of Chinese and Western Architectural Arts

洪坑村以方形客家土楼——崇裕楼、南昌楼为中心，向外围逐渐拓展，形成了由13座明代大型土楼和33座清代土楼共同构成的土楼群。它们于2008年7月被列入了《世界遗产名录》。

振成楼是村落土楼群里中西建筑艺术融合的杰出代表。

振成楼整体风格精致细腻，大胆而内敛，现代又传统。富丽堂皇的装饰构件及大门、内墙、祖庭、花墙都透着中西建筑艺术融合的气息。土楼中心是家族议事、会客、听戏的公共场所，更是建筑艺术的

集中体现。四层高的土楼，砖木外墙、雕刻精细的柱脚、木刻成画的门面、乳白石柱和琉璃瓦当，以及木制走廊栏杆上的"梅兰竹菊"四君子图案，共同形成了强烈的冲突美感。

振成楼陪伴村落百年，与人们朝夕相处，成为古老村落中最耀眼的存在。

Hongkeng Village is built around the square-shaped Chongyu Tulou and Nanchang Tulou. It is a Tulou cluster boasting 13 large Tulou sites of the Ming Dynasty and 33 Tulou sites of the Qing Dynasty, which have been inscribed into the *World Heritage List* in July 2008.

Among them, Zhencheng Tulou is a masterpiece of the combination of Chinese and Western architectural arts.

Walking into this Tulou, you will find the overall exquisite and delicate architectural style, and enjoy the bold yet introverted, modern yet traditional charm. The magnificent decorative components, the gates, the interior walls, the ancestral courtyards and the perforated walls, all reflect the perfect integration of Chinese and Western architectural arts. The center of the Tulou once served as a public place for family meetings, receptions and operas, and is also the best expression of the architectural art. The four-floor Tulou, with the brick-wood outer walls, the finely carved column bases, the carved wooden facade, the opal stone columns and the glazed tiles, as well as the patterns of the so-called "four gentlemen of Chinese flowers", namely, plum blossom, orchid, bamboo and chrysanthemum, on the wooden corridor railings, delivers a strong aesthetic felling of conflicts.

After hundreds of years, Zhencheng Tulou has been a glaring presence in the ancient village.

龙岩·永定岩太村
Yantai Village, Yongding County, Longyan City

 龙岩海拔最高的梯田和土楼群
The Highest Terraces and Tulou Cluster in Longyan City

　　岩太村西傍永定第一名山——东华山，东临奇石山，巍峨壮阔、连绵起伏的群山，遍野青翠，孕育了梯田，也包裹着土楼。

　　因为山，这里形成了极致的梯田景观，梯田坡度几乎为35度，从山脚盘绕到山顶，层层叠叠、依次错落。从高处望去，梯田一条条、一根根，或平行或交叉，优美的曲线像琴弦乐谱般动感撩人。

　　村落的46座方形、圆形土楼顺势而建，坐落在海拔750~900米的山腰上，同梯田一样，高低错落。它们是永定区海拔最高、规模最大的土楼群。其中，福龙楼是村落最古老的土楼。而福盛楼是最年轻的，也是最大的圆土楼，高峰时，曾有400余人在此居住。

每个清晨、雨后，村落都笼罩在茫茫的云雾中。山林氤氲的雾气，弥漫在梯田上、土楼里，更增添了村落的朦胧美和神秘感。

Yantai Village borders Donghua Mountain, the most famous mountain in Yongding County to the west, and Qishi Mountain to the east. Majestic and rolling mountains and green and lush fields are the places where Tulou cluster and surrounding terraces are developed.

Due to the mountainous features, an unbelievable terrace landscape came into being. The slope of the terraced fields is almost 35 degrees, which coil from the foot to the top of the mountains, layered and staggered one after another. Taking a bird's view, one will see the terraced fields aligned one by one, running parallel or across each other, giving shape to beautiful curves as enchanting as the musical strings and scores.

The 46 square and round-shaped Tulou in the village are located on the mountainside at an altitude of 750 to 900 meters. Like terraced fields, the buildings are also placed here and there all the way down. They are the highest and largest Tulou cluster in Yongding County. Among them, Fulong Tulou is the oldest earthen building in the village, while Fusheng Tulou is the youngest and largest round-shaped one. At its peak, over 400 people lived in Fusheng Tulou.

Every morning and after the rain, the village is shrouded in the clouds. Mist from the mountains and forests surrounds the terraces and the Tulou cluster, lending a touch of hazy beauty and mystery to the village.

龙岩·长汀三洲村
Sanzhou Village, Changting County, Longyan City

 水运码头上建起的村落
A Village Built on the Wharf

　　三洲村处在闽、赣、粤三省交界地，江河穿流而过。

　　依托独特的自然、地理条件，这里自唐末以来就是区域最重要的水运码头，也是连接三省的水陆交通枢纽。

　　水运码头上人头攒动，有"日见船帆不断,夜泊船桅成排"的热闹场景。为了服务往来人群，这里建成了商铺、公馆、驿站，逐渐形成了繁华的商

贸集市，进而孕育出了体系完整的商贸重镇。

如今，曾经的风云码头已成了江畔静候的传统村落。青砖黑瓦、石板小道，古朴而幽静。村落留存了戴氏家庙、戴氏民居群、风火屋、戴道宾祠、清代乾隆皇帝御笔书写的"古进贤乡"牌匾，为后人一遍遍地讲述着当年的繁荣景象。

Sanzhou Village is located at the junction of the three provinces of Fujian, Jiangxi and Guangdong, with Tingjiang River flowing through.

Due to the unique natural and geographical conditions, this place has been serving as the principal regional water transportation terminal since the Tang and the Song Dynasties. It also has been the land and water transportation hub connecting the three provinces.

The wharf used to be busy with crowds of people, presenting a scene of "sails come one after another by day, masts line up in a row at night." For the convenience of the comers and the goers, the village started to build shops, mansions and post stations. After years of development, it turned into a bustling bazaar and further translated itself into a full-fledged trade center.

Today, the once prosperous wharf has become an ancient village sitting tranquilly by the river. Gray bricks, black tiles, flagstone trails, among others, everything looks simple and quiet here. The village has preserved the Dai Family Ancestral Shrine, Dai Family Residence Cluster, Fenghuo House, Dai Daobin Shrine, and the plaque of "Gu Jin Xian Xiang" (Ancient Village, Home of Sages) written by the Qianlong Emperor of the Qing Dynasty. All these tell the past prosperity of the village to the later generations.

宁德

福安康源村	Kangyuan Village, Fu'an, Ningde City
福安廉村	Liancun Village, Fu'an, Ningde City
福安楼下村	Louxia Village, Fu'an, Ningde City
福安南岩村	Nanyan Village, Fu'an, Ningde City
福安坦洋村	Tanyang Village, Fu'an, Ningde City
福安秀峰村	Xiufeng Village, Fu'an, Ningde City
古田端上村	Duanshang Village, Gutian County, Ningde City
屏南北墘村	Beiqian Village, Pingnan County, Ningde City
屏南漈下村	Jixia Village, Pingnan County, Ningde City
寿宁下党村	Xiadang Village, Shouning County, Ningde City
霞浦半月里村	Banyueli Village, Xiapu County, Ningde City

宁德 · 福安康源村
Kangyuan Village, Fu'an, Ningde City

 《西游记》李靖的后世家族
Descendents of Li Jing, the Archetypal Character of the "Pagoda-Bearing Heavenly King" in *Journey to the West*

　　康源村李氏是唐代卫国公李靖的后裔。历史上，北方战乱，李氏家族从陕西三原县东里堡辗转千里到南方，于明代天顺年迁徙肇基康源村。

　　村落以"李"姓为主，有建于清代的李氏宗祠，以及供奉着先祖李靖夫妇的城隍庙。祠堂里一块块牌匾高悬，神坛里码放了94座雕刻精致的李氏家族祖宗牌位。座座牌位金碧辉煌，极其庄严。

如今,康源村在乡贤的带领下,把文化注入村落发展,形成了"李天王"品牌的龙虾养殖、传统黄酒酿造、百年芙蓉李、绿茶茶园等系列产业。这不仅弘扬了家族千年文化,也让村落遗产得到了活态传承。

The Li clan in Kangyuan Village is the descendants of Li Jing, a military commander in the Tang Dynasty. History shows that the Li family moved south from Donglibao Village in Sanyuan County, Shaanxi Province due to wars and conflicts in the north, and they ultimately settled in the village during Tianshun year of the Ming Dynasty.

With a majority of villagers surnamed Li, the village houses the Li Clan's Ancestral Hall built in the Qing Dynasty and a god temple for the lineage to worship their ancestors—Li Jing and his wife. Blessed with honorable plaques hung high up, the hall saves a designated space for an altar, where there are 94 exquisitely inscribed ancestral tablets placed in a magnificently solemn fashion.

Today, the well-respected have led the village in integrating distinct culture with its development, forming a series of industries under the brand name King Li, such as lobster breeding, rice wine brewing, Furong plum planting and green tea plantations. All these practices have not only renewed the millennium-old culture of the Li clan, but also translated it into tangible products.

宁德：福安廉村
Liancun Village, Fu'an, Ningde City

商埠码头与防御古堡
Commercial Port and Impregnable Fortress

廉村，成于穆阳溪。溪流孕育了肥沃的土地，也成就了村落的商贸地位。

唐代，穆阳溪即是水上交通要道，溪畔的廉村成了沟通闽东北与浙南的水陆枢纽。村南的商铺逐渐兴起，进而形成商埠古街，出现了"海舟鱼货并集，远通建宁府诸县"的繁华场景。

廉村终于成了中原世家大族南迁的理想定居地，也造就了"开闽第一进士村""一门五进士"的神话。

商文兼盛，富可敌国，这让外界垂涎。明嘉靖年间，为了防御猖獗的倭寇，腰缠万贯的廉村家族建造了环绕村落的古寨堡。寨堡设置了"廉、忠、孝、礼、义、信"六个寨门，坚不可摧，守护了村落百年。

如今，走在廉村，你需要细细品味其中的韵味，那是繁华之后的平淡，也是厚重之上的豁达。

Flowing through the ancient village of Liancun, the Muyang Stream has turned the land fertile and made the village a once-flourishing commercial hub.

As a critical watercourse in the Tang Dynasty, the Muyang Stream rendered its neighboring Liancun Village a business hub for transporting goods between northeastern Fujian and southern Zhejiang by water and land. With a variety of stores springing up, a bustling commercial street started taking shape and saw all sorts of goods delivered throughout northern Fujian.

The commercially dynamic village was then viewed by eminent families in Zhongyuan, the area on the lower reaches of the Yellow River, as an ideal place to live. Liancun Village was further recognized as the most-renowned village with Jinshi, or imperial scholars, in Fujian, and the tale about how five members in a household succeeded in the imperial examination and won the title of Jinshi has still been told today.

However, its developed economy and bustling entrepreneurial and cultural activities made it fall victim to invasion. During the Jiajing period of the Ming Dynasty, the affluent families in Liancun Village built a castle that had the village enclosed in a bid to guard against Japanese pirates. The castle has six gates, respectively named Lian (integrity), Zhong (loyalty), Xiao (filial piety), Li (etiquette), Yi (righteousness), and Xin (commitment), which are so strong that it is impossible to break into. This is why the village has been well-preserved for ages.

Today, while taking a stroll in the village, you can find the remaining charm, be it the peace after a splendid past, or the openness secured with formidable walls.

宁德·福安楼下村
Louxia Village, Fu'an, Ningde City

 ## 清代"豪宅"的聚集地
A Cluster of Ancient Mansions of the Qing Dynasty

楼下村周围群山环绕，时常云雾缭绕，天山共一色。弥漫的雾气间，清代大型古厝群遗存颇为壮观。

其中，坪中厝是楼下村刘氏家族的发迹地，最为知名。清嘉庆年间，刘家先祖建造了这座大厝。在宁德地区，它算得上大型豪宅。宅内多进，楹联颇多，雕刻精美。厅堂两侧都有"塾厅"，供昔日读书人静修用功。

厅堂中庭上方、左右两侧安插了神龛祖堂，这是家族最神圣的地方，故雕刻也最为精致。

随着后代繁衍，清嘉庆至咸丰的45年间，以垾中厝为核心，周边又陆续建造了30多幢形制相近的大宅，它们彼此紧密相邻，有石板巷道穿插其中。座座古宅有"青砖小瓦马头墙"的风韵，高低错落，气势非凡。

Surrounded by misty mountains, Louxia Village is home to an imposing cluster of ancient cuos built in the Qing Dynasty.

The most renowned among them is Yangzhongcuo Mansion, where the Liu clan in the village rose to fame. During the Jiaqing period of the Qing Dynasty, the ancestors of the Liu lineage built the majestic house, one of the largest in Ningde. The building has multiple doors decorated with exquisitely engraved couplets, and its hall is flanked by dedicated rooms for the literate to read and learn. Above the hall's courtyard and on both flanks are places for ancestral tablets boasting the most skillfully-created engravings as a way to signify solemnity.

For 45 years since the establishment, the Liu clan had built a total of over 30 similar mansions around the Yangzhongcuo Mansion. They are closely adjacent and linked by a network of stone-paved alleys. These houses, disproportionately arranged though, are imposing with a blend of gray bricks, small roof tiles, and horse head walls.

宁德·福安南岩村
Nanyan Village, Fu'an, Ningde City

育人为先的"书香门第"
A Historic Village that Values Education

　　700年前，王氏祖先们在南岩村种下的红柯树，至今仍守护着这一方水土，保佑着村落子嗣，见证着村落的古今荣耀。

　　村落以宗祠为中心，依山顺水分布着王氏先民建于明朝、清朝和民国的42座传统古厝。这些古厝均建有高宽门楼、前后天井、宽敞堂屋和左右厢房，它们梁柱粗大，辉绿岩柱础、屏风、斗拱、窗格上都有精美雕刻或彩绘，栩栩如生。民居连同古水井、古牌匾、古楹联、古方桌、古案台、古石门等多样的历史环境要素，共同赋予了南岩村"闽东明清建筑博物馆"的美誉。

　　"闽东明清建筑博物馆"中的王氏家族古厝里，还收藏着一副清同治年间的寿屏。这副寿屏上精细雕刻的500字，讲述了清代王氏家族重视教育，不惜重金请来先生，在家办私塾的故事。

Seven centuries on, the Lithocarpus fenzelianus trees planted by the ancestors of the Wang clan in Nanyan Village, remain impressively luxuriant as they stand as guards of the village, protecting its people while witnessing its glory of the past and today.

Centering on the ancestral hall, the village is home to 42 featured cuos built by the forefathers of the Wang lineage in the Ming and Qing Dynasties, some in the period of the Republic of China in Chinese mainland. These ancient buildings feature a high and wide gate tower, front and back courtyards, spacious halls, and wing-rooms on both sides. With boughs as their beams and pillars, they couldn't be more alive with the exquisite engravings and paintings on rock plinths, screens, corbel brackets, and window screens. Along with that, the ancient facilities and items—wells, plaques, couplets, square and rectangular tables, stone doors, etc. have won Nanyan Village the fame of "Architecture Museum of the Ming and Qing Dynasties in eastern Fujian."

In the age-old cuo of the Wang family lies a birthday celebration screen of the Tongzhi period in the Qing Dynasty inscribed with an intriguing story in just 500 Chinese characters, which tells about how the Wang clan in the Qing Dynasty valued education and invited respected tutors for homeschooling at a high price.

181 / Traditional Villages in Fujian

宁德·福安坦洋村
Tanyang Village, Fu'an, Ningde City

 以"坦洋工夫茶"名扬天下的村落
A Village Famous for Tanyang Congou

"喝过坦洋工夫茶，人走情常在。"这是20世纪80年代，时任宁德地委书记的习近平四进坦洋村调研，带领坦洋村村民大面积种植茶树时留下的感慨。

坦洋村坐落于世界地质公园白云山东麓，900米的高海拔造就了"晴天早晚遍地雾，阴雨终日满山云"的景观，独特的自然环境非常适宜茶树生长。于是，明代洪武年间，坦洋人便开始种植茶树。直到清咸丰年间，坦洋工夫茶终于形

成稳定的工艺，并于1915年荣获巴拿马万国博览会金奖，扬名四海。

坦洋村因"工夫茶"而兴，这里是茶的王国：有坦洋工夫茶创始人施光凌的老宅，有茶叶交易场所真武廊桥，有茶农上茶山时躲雨避风的观音桥，有茶行旧址横楼，有祈求茶商水上平安的妈祖庙，有承接闽东13县茶叶运输的古官道，还有防匪患保安全的碉楼炮台。鼎盛时期，村落有胡氏"万兴隆"、施氏"兴泰隆"等近36家茶行，至今很多茶行仍开张迎客。

"After drinking Tanyang Congou, one will always miss the village when one has left." In the 1980s, Xi Jinping, then Secretary of the CPC Ningde Prefectural Committee, made the remark in relation to a campaign he was promoting to get local people to grow the special tea.

Tanyang village is located in the Baiyunshan World Geopark, the altitude of 900 meters creates a landscape of fog even all day long on sunny days and clouds on rainy days—a unique environment which is beneficial to the growth of tea trees. It was during the Hongwu period of the Ming Dynasty that Tanyang people began tea planting. By the Xianfeng period of the Qing Dynasty, Tanyang Congou finally achieved a stable craftsmanship, enabling it to win a gold medal at the Panama World Expo in 1915, thus bringing it international fame.

Tanyang Village has long been famous for its Tanyang Congou, and it is the Kingdom of Tea. There are old residence of Shi Guangling, the tea founder of Tanyang Congou, the Zhenwu Corridor Bridge, a tea trading market, the Guanyin Bridge serving as a shelter from rain and winds for the tea farmers, Henglou, an old tea shop site, the Mazu Temple where people pray for the safety of tea traders on the high seas, the ancient official road for tea transportation in the 13 counties in eastern Fujian, and the guard towers and turrets built to prevent banditry and ensure public safety. In its heyday, there were nearly 36 tea shops in the village, including Hu's Wanxinglong and Shi's Xingtailong, and many are still open today.

宁德·福安秀峰村
Xiufeng Village, Fu'an, Ningde City

 田园秘境中的朴素人家
Simple Families in the Quiet Countryside

秀峰村从古至今都隐秘在钟灵毓秀的山峰间。人们早起迎晨光，傍晚送夕阳，过着朴素的田园生活，也守候着家族的兴旺。

村落背靠青山，面朝晓汾溪水，大片竹林、百亩茶园、秀峰人家、清澈溪流，共同构成了一幅富有层次美感的田园村居图。

鹅卵石铺就的蜿蜒小道，串联起了座座夯土老屋。秀峰村的百年老屋是闽东典型的三合院，以晓汾溪中的鹅卵石筑墙基，用林中的木材做房屋框架，取地上的黏土夯成坚实的墙，没有太过繁复的装饰，只有朴实无华的韵味。

几百年间，人们对神灵与祖先的敬畏始终如一，对家族繁盛的追求不断。每家每户都会在房屋正厅两侧门的上方供奉神灵与祖先牌位，左边祭祀神灵，右边祭奠先祖。正厅两侧的木墙、木柱上更是张贴了条条红色的楹联和庆贺词，十分喜庆。人们以这种方式，珍藏了家族不同时期的喜庆之事，也昭示着家族的代代繁荣。

Traditional Villages in Fujian

Xiufeng Village has been hidden among the beautiful mountains since ancient times. People there have always lived a simple rural life, greeting the rising sun in the morning and watching the sunset in the evening. They work hard in pursuit of a good life.

The village is backed by green hills, facing Xiaofen Stream, and has abundant bamboo groves, and nearly seven hectares of tea gardens. Houses dot the slope rising from the bank of the stream, forming an idyllic setting with rich aesthetic beauty.

A winding path paved with pebbles connects the century-old rammed earth houses, which represent the typical courtyard with houses on three sides in eastern Fujian province. It the houses are built with pebbles taken from the Xiaofen Stream, with wood felled from the forest providing the frame of the house, and clay taken from the ground rammed into solid walls. There isn't much complicated decoration, only plain charm.

For hundreds of years, people's reverence for gods and their own ancestors has been consistent, along with the perpetual pursuit of family prosperity. Each family sets up memorial tablets for both gods and ancestors above the doors on both sides of the main hall—gods tablets on the left and ancestors tablets on the right. The wooden walls and pillars on both sides of the main hall are also pasted with festive red couplets and congratulatory messages. In this way, people cherish the celebrations of the family at different times, and also show the prosperity of the family from generation to generation.

宁德·古田端上村
Duanshang Village, Gutian County, Ningde City

爱国高僧圆瑛法师故里
Hometown of Patriotic Master Yuanying

端上村是高僧圆瑛法师的出生地。他一生倡导和平，抗日战争期间，曾七下南洋为抗战开展募捐活动。1949年后，他被推选为中国佛教协会首任会长，是公认的佛教界领袖。

如今，端上村仍保留了很多与圆瑛法师相关的传统建筑与风俗。村落有建于明末的圆瑛故居、圆瑛小时候就读的私塾、圆瑛捐资修建的圆瑛学堂等，还会定期举行圆瑛法师纪念活动，吸引各界人士参与、

祭拜。圆瑛故居也被辟为"宁德市爱国主义教育基地"。

当你行走在村中，既能感受其中的古朴与韵味，亦能追忆起圆瑛法师的爱国故事。

Duanshang Village is the birthplace of Master Yuanying, who advocated peace throughout his life. He made seven voyages to Southeast Asia to raise funds for the War of Resistance Against Japanese Aggression. After 1949, he was elected the first president of the Buddhist Association of China and recognized as a leader of the Buddhist community in China.

Today, Duanshang Village still retains many traditional buildings and customs related to Master Yuanying. The village has the former residence of Yuanying built in the late Ming Dynasty, the private school where Yuanying studied and the Yuanying Academy funded by him. There are regular activities commemorating Master Yuanying in the village, attracting people from all walks of life for participation and worship. Yuanying's former residence was also established as Patriotic Education Base of Ningde City.

Walking in the village, one can feel its simplicity and charm and recall the patriotic story of Master Yuanying.

宁德 · 屏南北墘村
Beiqian Village, Pingnan County, Ningde City

 百年老酒"酿造"出的村落
A Village Best Known for its Time-honored Wine Culture

600多年来，北墘村始终传承不变的是"北墘黄酒"。

北墘村是红曲与黄酒的著名产地。村落制曲业始于明代，盛于清代。当时，几乎家家户户都生产红曲，产品行销上海、浙江以及东南亚等地。

制曲与酿酒业的发达，造就了一批酒商巨贾。他们掷金千两，造房修路，建设村落。北墘村精致的佛仔厝、釉埕、吴氏宗祠、郑公桥、攀龙桥及纵横的街巷都是明清时期逐渐建成的，它们共同构成了北墘人的生产、生活环境。

此外，北墘村亦建有哨楼、炮楼用于防御。哨楼在街巷尽头，分

两层，上层可窥探匪徒，下层关门即可挡住侵扰。炮楼在村落外围，建于丛林掩蔽的制高点，高达20多米，也有防御匪徒之用。

如今，北墘村通过传承、创新黄酒技艺，将"北墘黄酒"再次推向世界，也让村落文化得到了广泛传播。

For the past six centuries and more, the Beiqian Village has stayed committed to brewing "Beiqian Rice Wine".

Beiqian Village is a famous producing area of red yeast rice and rice wine, and the village started to produce red yeast rice, a type of fermentation starter, in the Ming Dynasty and the industry flourished in the Qing Dynasty. At that time, nearly all households in the village produced the red yeast rice and sold it to Shanghai, Zhejiang, and even Southeast Asia.

The bustling starter-making and winemaking industries enriched a host of businessmen and wine vendors, naturally. And because of their generosity, the village was more alive with newly-built houses and roads. The delicately-designed architecture, such as Fozai Cuo Mansion, Qucheng (a large workshop for making red yeast rice), Wu Clan's Ancestral Hall,

Zhenggong Bridge, Panlong Bridge, and a crisscross network of alleys, was completed in the Ming and Qing Dynasties and has shaped the way the villagers live and work.

To defend it from invaders, the village also built a watchtower and a blockhouse. The watchtower was built at the end of the alley. There are two stories in the watchtower, with the upper one for observing intended intruders, who can be shut out by the gate on the lower floor. However, the blockhouse, over 20 meters high, was constructed on the periphery of the village where guardians can hide in jungle to ambush bandits.

By promoting and innovating winemaking techniques, the village has spread the Beiqian Rice Wine together with its distinct culture throughout the globe.

宁德·屏南漈下村
Jixia Village, Pingnan County, Ningde City

 ## 传世廊桥与多元彩绘
Ancient Corridor Bridge and Multicolored Painting

漈下村位于"中国木拱廊桥文化之乡"屏南下辖的甘棠乡,是世界非物质文化遗产——"中国木拱桥传统营造技艺"的代表地。廊桥,是一种"桥上建廊,以廊护桥,桥廊一体"的独特桥梁形式,是中国木结构桥梁的典型代表。《清明上河图》中的汴水虹桥就是一座虹状木桥,而处于多水地区的漈下村廊桥,则在虹状木桥上增加廊屋,保护桥梁免受雨水侵蚀。

贯穿村落的水街由两溪汇聚而成,村头水口、村中心和村尾处建有三座木拱廊桥:广通桥、迎仙桥和聚宝桥。它们是过河的通道,也是全村聚会的场所。廊桥内设有神龛以奉祀神祇,保佑全村平安。

廊桥之外,村落不同时代的遗存颇多,有明代甘氏家族迁徙于此后修筑的城墙、城楼、炮楼和练兵场;有漈下村作为交通枢纽而形成的条条古驿道、接待达官贵人的官厅厝、供远途行人歇脚的峙国亭;有供奉福建女性神灵马仙娘的龙漈仙宫;还有甘氏宗祠,保佑全村平安的飞来庙,以及刻满了革命年代、大生产时代红色标语的旧公所。大多数遗存内的彩绘壁画也各具鲜明的特色。

Jixia Village is located in Gantang Township under the jurisdiction of Pingnan, the "Hometown of Chinese Wooden Arch Bridge Culture." It is a home to the world's intangible cultural heritage—traditional design and practices for building Chinese wooden arch bridges. As a typical representative of wooden bridges in China, is a unique wooden bridge with a corridor built on. The bridge over the Bian River in the famous ancient panoramic painting *Qingming Shanghe Tu* (*Along the River during the Qingming Festival*) is a wooden arch one. Given the plentiful rain in Jixia Village, a corridor is added on the wooden arch bridge to protect it from rain erosion.

The water street running through the village is formed by the convergence of two streams. Three wooden arch bridges were built at the entrance, in the middle and at the end of the village, namely Guangtong Bridge, Yingxian Bridge and Jubao Bridge. They are not only passages across the waterway but also

gathering places of the whole village. There is a shrine in each corridor bridge for worshiping various gods and praying for the peace of the village.

Besides the corridor bridges, there are many remains of different times to be found here, such as the city walls, gate towers, turrets and training grounds built by the Gan family in the Ming Dynasty after their migration from elsewhere; the ancient post roads, the official reception hall for visiting dignitaries, and the Zhiguo Pavilion for the long-distance travelers to rest— all formed when the village served as a transportation hub; the Dragon Palace worshiping the beautiful female deity Ma Xiangu, the Gan clan's Ancestral Hall, the Feilai Temple safeguarding village safety; the site of old government offices where one see many red slogans on walls, which are the product of the revolutionary years and the Great Leap Forward Campaign. The painted murals in most of the remains also have distinct characteristics.

宁德：寿宁下党村
Xiadang Village, Shouning County, Ningde City

 闽浙交界地带的"中国第一古廊桥"
"China's NO.1 Ancient Corridor Bridge" at the Junction of Fujian and Zhejiang

下党村处在闽浙交界地带，因溪水川流百年，绵长不息而得名"党川"，后更名为"下党"。溪流之上，始建于明代的鸾峰桥，自古便是闽浙通道。它是寿宁廊桥的代表，是全国现存单拱跨度最大的木拱廊桥，也是东南险桥之一。

廊桥上覆双坡顶，两旁加雨披，一端的桥台依托自然悬崖凿成，另一端的桥台用山上的石块砌筑。桥内的雕刻朴实无华，却有深厚的历史、文化底蕴。桥中央的神龛中供奉着福建民间崇奉的女神——临水夫人，长年香火旺盛。

百年里，廊桥与村落一起，见证了特殊年代的历史。土地革命战争时期，老一辈革命家领导的革命队伍就经常由鸾峰桥，往来于闽浙两省进行革命活动，并在廊桥上遮风避雨。20世纪80年代，廊桥更是见证了时任宁德地委书记的习近平跋山涉水到下党村现场办公、带领乡亲脱贫的故事。

鸾峰桥已于2006年被公布为"全国重点文物保护单位"，其营造技艺，即"中国木拱桥传统营造技艺"也被联合国教科文组织纳入了《急需保护的非物质文化遗产目录》。

Xiadang Village is located at the junction of Fujian and Zhejiang. It was named "Dangchuan" because of the endless flow of the Xiadang Stream for hundreds of years, and later renamed "Xiadang." Above the stream is the Luanfeng Bridge built in the Ming Dynasty, a channel connecting Fujian and Zhejiang since ancient times. It represents the artistry of corridor bridges in Shouning County, the "Hometown of Corridor Bridges." It is also the largest single-arched wooden corridor bridge in China, and one of the bridges located above dangerous streams in southeast China.

The bridge is covered with double sloped-roofs and rainproof covers on both sides. One of the bridge abutment is chiseled against a natural cliff, and the other is built with stones from the mountain. The sculptures in the bridge are simple, but with rich historical and cultural background. The shrine in the middle of the bridge enshrines Goddess Linshui, a deity admired by the people of Fujian, and it has been frequently worshipped

throughout the years.

In the past century, the corridor bridge, along with the village, have witnessed ups and downs in the history of a special era. During the Agrarian Revolutionary War, the revolutionary team led by the older generation of revolutionists often traveled between Fujian and Zhejiang provinces for revolutionary activities through the Luanfeng Bridge, and took shelter against wind and rain on the corridor bridge. In the 1980s, the corridor bridge witnessed how Xi Jinping, then secretary of the CPC Ningde Prefectural Committee, traveled across mountains and rivers to Xiadang Village and led the villagers out of poverty.

Luanfeng Bridge was listed as one of the National key Cultrual Relics Protection Units in 2006. Besides, the "traditional construction techniques of wooden arch bridges" , a construction technique adopted to the building of the Lunafeng Bridge, has been listed in the "*List of Intangible Cultural Heritage in Need of Urgent Safeguarding*" by UNESCO.

宁德·霞浦半月里村
Banyueli Village, Xiapu County, Ningde City

大山里的商贸古村
An Ancient Commercial Center in the Mountains

半月里村,因恰处于霞浦县城通往霞浦东吾洋的古官道中段而得名。依托交通枢纽位置,这个周围山峦起伏、林壑幽深、碧水徊环的畲族古寨,竟也曾因商贸而繁盛。

清雍正年间,雷世茂带领乡亲将畲山上的茶叶通过古道、东吾洋外销,又将布匹、金银等货物带回了畲乡。如今的雷世茂故居仍述说着当年的辉煌,雕梁画栋、镂空细刻,精致万分,126根木柱气势磅礴。为了保佑村落的平安,古宅砖墙的空斗缝隙间,还塞满了河中取来的鹅卵石,作为抵御盗贼的武器。

商贸也影响了村落的信仰。龙溪宫中,不仅供奉了畲族民间信仰的神祇薛仁贵元

帅、陈九郎元帅、平水明王杨从仪和雷万春元帅，还供奉着保佑全村茶叶出海顺利的妈祖娘娘。

　　传统的商贸时代虽已远去，但畲族村寨的特色得以保留。永庆寺、雷氏宗祠、举人府、秀才院、3座清代大型青砖"豪宅"，以及枝繁叶茂的古榕树群、30多座明清杰出人物的大墓留存至今；被纳入国家级非物质文化遗名录的畲族婚俗、畲族小说歌，还在这里一直传承、传唱着。

Banyueli Village got its name because it was right in the middle of the ancient official road from the town to Dongwuyang of Xiapu County. Thanks to its location as a transportation hub, this She ethnic village surrounded by rolling hills, dense forests and clear waters, prospered as a commercial center.

During Emperor Yongzheng's reign in the Qing Dynasty, Lei Shimao led the villagers to export the tea on She Mountain through the ancient road and Dongwuyang, and brought back to the village such goods as cloth, gold and silver. Today Lei, Shimao's former residence still displays the glory of the past, with 126 magnificent wooden pillars showing exquisite hollowed-out carvings and paintings. To protect the village from thieves, gaps between the brick walls of the ancient houses were filled with cobblestones.

Commerce and trade also influenced the villagers' beliefs. In the Longxi Palace, the deities worshipped include not only Marshal Xue Rengui, Marshal Chen Jiulang, Marshal Yang Congyi, and Marshal Lei Wanchun who are gods in folklore of the She people, but also the goddess Mazu who blessed the villagers for tea trade along the sea routes.

Though the days of commerce and trade are gone, distinct features of the She ethnic village are preserved. Yongqing Temple, Lei Clan's Ancestral Hall, Juren Mansion, Xiucai Courtyard, three large-scale brick-made "mansions" dating back to the Qing Dynasty, as well as lush ancient banyan trees and over 30 tombs of outstanding figures in the Ming and Qing Dynasties have been preserved to this day. She people's wedding customs and novel songs, included in the National Intangible Cultural Heritage List, are still carried forward and sung here.

蜗 平潭

北港村　Beigang Village, Pingtan
青峰村　Qingfeng Village, Pingtan

平潭 · 北港村
Beigang Village, Pingtan

 山海"会盟"的文创村

A Village of Culture and Creativity Surrounded by Mountains and Sea

北港村位于平潭岛东部，背靠群山，面朝海湾。

碧海、蓝天、座座码头和241座石头厝共同造就了顶级的风光美景，这让北港村从百年的小渔村，一跃成为现代的文创地。

作为平潭综合实验区、国际旅游岛的重要组成部分，北港村用海一样的胸怀，为海峡两岸年轻人提供了造梦空间。他们依托这里独特的自然、人文资源优势，在保护碧海银滩等宝贵资源的同时，对原生态的山、石、田、海的开发利用发挥到了极致。如今，村落逐渐形成了以山海、民居为内涵的文创、观光和休闲产业，成了原生态海岛渔村文化旅游目的地和远近闻名的文创村。

Situated in the eastern Pingtan Island, Beigang Village is blessed with imposing mountains and an inviting bay.

Joined by a picturesque view featuring blue skies and azure waters, coupled with multiple piers and 241 featured stone cuos, Beigang Village has morphed from a century-old fishing village into a modern community of culture and creativity.

As an integral part of the Pingtan Comprehensive Experimental Zone and the International Tourism Island, the village welcomes young people from both sides of the Taiwan Straits and offers them everything they need to start their career. Relying on the unique natural and cultural resources, they stay committed to the proper protection and development of its natural treasures.

Nowadays, the village has seen the emergence of the cultural, creative, sight-seeing, and leisure industries underpinned by the fascinating natural landscape and rows of distinctive residential houses, making it a tourist destination known not just for the ecological environment but also for its pursuit of cultural creativity.

平潭 · 青峰村
Qingfeng Village, Pingtan

 世代以捕鱼为生的海岛渔村
An Island Village that Lives on Fishing for Generations

青峰村位于福建平潭岛北端，是一座三面环海的小渔村。这里的一切都与海洋有关。

明代，从中原迁徙于此的刘氏家族，利用滨海优势，开始以捕鱼为生。为了保佑家人出海平安，青峰村人会定期祭拜神灵。村落遗存的清代大王宫和青峰寺内，壁画精致、雕梁画栋，寄托了面朝大海的人们对美好生活的向往。

因为临海，村落时常遭遇台风侵袭。能抵御台风的石头厝民居渐成特色。石头厝就地取材，山上的土、海中的石、林中的木，都是它的建造材料。房顶上用石头压着瓦片，也起到了防风暴的作用。这种石头厝在平潭岛有近4万栋，而青峰村则是主要集中地之一。

如今，青峰村有近18艘大型捕鱼船，常年倚在海上，与蔚蓝的天空、深邃的大海共同构成了一道亮丽的海洋风景线。每到日出，渔民都会迎着晨光走向海洋，成群结队的身影淹没在了大片沙滩中。

Situated at the northern tip of Pingtan Island, Fujian, the small fishing village of Qingfeng is surrounded on three sides by water. Everything here is related to the sea.

The Liu clan migrated from Zhongyuan, an area on the lower reaches of the Yellow River, to the village in the Ming Dynasty before fishing for a living. To secure for those going to sea the full blessings of deities, villagers hold regular worship coromonies. The Dawang Palace and Qingfeng Temple in the village, both built in the Qing Dynasty, remain alive with the beauty of exquisite wall paintings, engraved beams, and painted ridgepoles, from which we can see the locals, pursuit of a better life.

The proximity to the sea, however, makes the village vulnerable to seasonal typhoons. To guard against the natural threat, the locals built stone cuos with such local materials as mountain soils, sea stones, and lumber, while pressing against tiles with rocks. Pingtan Island is now home to nearly 40,000 featured stone cuos, and Qingfeng Village is one of the main centers of stone cuos.

Today, the village has a total of about 18 large fishing vessels at sea all year round. Joined by blue sky and boundless sea, these ships make for a stunning skyline. At dawn, hordes of fishermen would head out to sea, greeting a yellow glow of sunlight and, slowly, moving out of sight in golden sands.

党的十八大以来，以习近平同志为核心的党中央高度重视文化建设，鲜明地提出了文化自信，它与道路自信、理论自信、制度自信一同被列为中国特色社会主义的"四个自信"，开辟了弘扬中国精神、中国文化的新境界。

传统村落保护的主旨正是传承传统文化，唤醒公众的文化自信。自 2013 年起，每年中央 1 号文件均提出了传统村落保护的相关要求。2017 年，中共中央办公厅、国务院办公厅印发了《关于实施中华优秀传统文化传承发展工程的意见》，将弘扬传统村落优秀文化、传统村落保护工程列为重要目标。

中国城市规划设计研究院积极响应国家号召，投入传统村落保护的各项工作中，既有落地实践，也有价值传播。中国城市规划设计研究院于 2017 年配合中国住房和城乡建设部组织编写了《走近中国传统村落》，于 2020 年组织编写了《走近福建传统村落》，逐步形成了全国传统村落价值挖掘、文化传播的系列画册。

此次编写《走近福建传统村落》画册，得到了福建省住房和城乡建设厅的大力支持。在画册主题定位、传统村落价值提炼等方面，得到了住建厅林瑞良厅长、蒋金明副厅长、苏友佺总经济师的亲切指导；在传统村落筛选、地方对接、内容质量把关等方面，得到了住建厅风貌办许勇铁主任、林琼华副主任、黄敏敏副主任及潘一翔、林楚修、

Since the 18th National Congress of the Communist Party of China (CPC) in 2012, the CPC Central Committee with Comrade Xi Jinping at its core has given priority to cultural progress by making out a case for strong confidence in the path, theory, system and culture of socialism with Chinese characteristics. That suggests a new way for China to promote its philosophy and culture.

The protection of traditional villages is designed to inherit traditional culture and enable the general public to be more confident in their culture. The task has been a priority in the annual No.1 central document since 2013. *The Suggestions on Implementation of Projects to Promote and Develop Excellent Traditional Chinese Culture*, issued by the General Office of the CPC Central Committee and the General Office of the State Council in 2017, considers it a goal of great significance to protect traditional villages and promote fine culture.

To respond to the call, the China Academy of Urban Planning and Design has participated in various projects aimed to protect traditional villages. For one thing, practices have been adopted in this respect; for another, the value of these villages has been delivered. In 2017, the Academy supported China's Ministry of Housing and Urban-Rural Development in compiling the book *Traditional Villages in China*. In 2020, it prepared the photo album *Traditional Villages in Fujian*, complementing the album series that identify and promote the value of traditional Chinese villages.

The Department of Housing and Urban-Rural Development of Fujian provided substantial support for the development of the photo album. Guidance on how to present the album's theme and identify the value of traditional villages was given by the Department's director Lin Ruiliang, deputy director Jiang Jinming, and chief economist Su Youquan. And Xu Yongtie, head of the Architectural Landscape Office of the Department, the Office's deputy head Lin Qionghua and Huang Minmin, Pan Yixiang, Lin Chuxiu, Shen Siyu, Lin Qi, and other personnel concerned assisted us with the selection of villages, connection to local authorities, and

沈思宇、林祺等同志的帮助，在此深表感谢。

在50个传统村落的实地调研、采访、拍摄过程中，特别感谢福州、漳州、泉州、三明、莆田、南平、龙岩、宁德、平潭等地市区、县住建局，以及相应地方乡镇人民政府的全力配合，感谢地方村落村民的积极参与。

画册收录了福建50个传统村落精美的摄影图片，既有各传统村落航拍、平面图片，也有村落独特的自然环境、传统建筑、风土人情图片，它们出自各地摄影师之手。正是对文化的热爱，激发了摄影师们对传统村落之美的感知。他们用独特的视角发现了传统的韵味，以专业的光影技术记录了村落的故事，使画册更加流光溢彩，更能触动读者的感情。

在此，需要感谢的摄影师有：高长清、胡家新、陈军、苏建强、李艺爽、徐敬宏、林致凡、颜家蔚、陈晨殷、钟鹰、林民良、倪政榕、林和安、林少锋、王维平、温学元、张培奋、陈成才、张梓昌、张艺欣、陈金标、陈怡建、黄文斌、林跃、颜志发、张晓美、詹彦彪、吴新华、郭燕鹏、黄少阳、王德概、张泉春、朱志雄、许少华、林光儿、罗联永、邓英强、周雄、陈纪凤、黄在锦、陈奇、杨孝庆、张志坚、张宗铝、黄三定、杨为春、林杜鸿、卓育兴、范思哲、邹建军、温桂芳、张庆文、吴心正、陈美中、翁斌、施惠清、邹义东、王福平、翁武财、叶劲峰、林艺谋、厦冰、张剑辉、李哲文、葛缨冠、廖清平、谢勤杰、杨婉娴、高志坚、林森鑫、李金文、黄守晟、陈崇焕、叶林生、林辉、郑品官、郑献兴、张耀辉、刘志群、董红。

在画册出版过程中，也得到了北京出版集团的大力支持，在此一并表示感谢。

quality control of contents. We are grateful for the hard work of these figures.

As we carried out the research, set up interviews, and took photos in the 50 traditional villages in Fujian, we also enjoyed support from the construction bureaus of cities and counties, including Fuzhou, Zhangzhou, Quanzhou, Sanming, Putian, Nanping, Longyan, Ningde, and Pingtan, and the relevant governments of townships, as well as villagers involved, for which we are deeply appreciative.

The photo album presents stunning photos of 50 traditional villages in Fujian taken by photographers across China. More than about the aerial view of villages in general, the photos particularly show their natural landscape, historical buildings, and local customs. It is the passion for culture of all kinds that inspires photographers to explore the beauty of traditional villages. The illustrated album can stir special emotions as photographers from a unique perspective capture the traditional nuance rooted from the villages and document the story behind them in a professional way.

We want to express our heartfelt thanks to these photographers, including Gao Changqing, Hu Jiaxin, Chen Jun, Su Jianqiang, Li Yishuang, Xu Jinghong, Lin Zhifan, Yan Jiawei, Chen Chenyin, Zhong Ying, Lin Minliang, Ni Zhengrong, Lin He'an, Lin Shaofeng, Wang Weiping, Wen Xueyuan, Zhang Peifen, Chen Chengcai, Zhang Zichang, Zhang Yixin, Chen Jinbiao, Chen Yijian, Huang Wenbin, Lin Yue, Yan Zhifa, Zhang Xiaomei, Zhan Yanbiao, Wu Xinhua, Guo Yanpeng, Huang Shaoyang, Wang Degai, Zhang Quanchun, Zhu Zhixiong, Xu Shaohua, Lin Guang'er, Luo Lianyong, Deng Yingqiang, Zhou Xiong, Chen Jifeng, Huang Zaijin, Chen Qi, Yang Xiaoqing, Zhang Zhijian, Zhang Zonglv, Huang Sanding, Yang Weichun, Lin Duhong, Zhuo Yuxing, Fan Sizhe, Zou Jianjun, Wen Guifang, Zhang Qingwen, Wu Xinzheng, Chen Meizhong, Weng Bin, Shi Huiqing, Zou Yidong, Wang Fuping, Weng Wucai, Ye Jinfeng, Lin Yimou, Xia Bing, Zhang Jianhui, Li Zhewen, Ge Yingguan, Liao Qingping, Xie Qinjie, Yang Wanxian, Gao Zhijian, Lin Senxin, Li Jinwen, Huang Shousheng, Chen Chonghuan, Ye Linsheng, Lin Hui, Zheng Pinguan, Zheng Xianxing and Zhang Yaohui, Liu Zhiqun, Dong Hong.

Many thanks also go to Beijing Publishing Group for its great support in publishing the photo album.